Jesus said that it would be better for his followers for him to go away. Why? Because, he said, he would send the Holy Spirit who would convict the world of sin and righteousness. This book will help guide earnest Christians into a deeper understanding of the person and work of the Holy Spirit, and it will be a blessing to many.

Tom McCall
Timothy C. and Julie M. Tennent Chair of Theology
Asbury Theological Seminary

Nothing thrills me more than holding a book that has spent its pages glorying in the holiness, the transcendence, the beauty of our magnificent God. With this book, Matt Ayars has laid a proper stage in discussions of Scripture and the historical record, and then he has offered that stage to the Holy Spirit, inviting us to gaze on grace and truth and enter into his freedom. Help has arrived, Ayars assures us, and this is very good news!

Carolyn Moore
founding pastor of Mosaic Church

Holy Spirit: An Introduction is a rich doctrinal study that is both deep and wide in its approach and appeal. Doctrine is for the people, not just the scholar. The book explores the depths and mystery of the Holy Spirit, covering the extensive operations of the Spirit in a way that carries gravity, yet is accessible to all readers to enter into fruitful conversation and holy living. Scriptural, theological, sound, accessible, and applicable. I deeply appreciated the sections on the Trinity and the gifts of the Spirit—rigorous, yet practical. There is much talk in our day about the Holy Spirit—many voices but some not so definitive and clear as Dr. Ayars in this volume. I recommend it as an excellent devotional resource for clergy and lay people, as well as for small-group study.

Peter J. Bellini
professor of church renewal and evangelization in the Heisel Chair
United Theological Seminary, Dayton, Ohio

The Holy Spirit has been the most misunderstood or neglected member of the Trinity for too long. Matt Ayars's book on the Holy Spirit is a concise yet thorough introduction to the person and work of the Holy Spirit. This is a needed and welcomed contribution for the church. I highly recommend this book!

Kevin Watson
Director of Academic Growth and Formation
Asbury Theological Seminary

One seldom encounters a book on the Spirit that intimately conjoins theology and actual life as that found in this remarkable distillation of the personalizing presence of the Holy Spirit. Matt Ayars clearly lays out the biblical, consensual, and orthodox materials with a view to making every theological point regarding the Spirit applicable to lived experience. Anyone desiring to know the Holy Spirit more intimately or to dive into what he offers to every believer will find this book more than helpful. I do not know a book on the Spirit that is clearer on the full salvation which the indwelling Spirit affords. Here is a robust and comprehensive understanding of how the transformative, victorious presence of the Spirit personally deals with all sin and powerfully enables persons to embody holy love.

Bill Ury
international ambassador for holiness
Salvation Army

Matt Ayars has written a beautiful account of the person and work of the Holy Spirit. While his work probes the depths of biblical and theological teaching on the Holy Spirit, he writes in a way that is accessible to both clergy and laity. This book is for the student preparing for ministry, as well as the Christian who desires to grow in faith. It is an invitation to participation in the holy life of God through the Holy Spirit. Ayars writes with an eye to the best of historical reflection on the Spirit, while at the same time making it a means of justifying, sustaining, and sanctifying grace. It is theology that leads to doxology—the praise and awe of God.

Chris Bounds
professor of theology and dean of the School of Theology and Ministry
Indiana Wesleyan University

Matt Ayars's *The Holy Spirit: An Introduction* provides an academically sound yet very readable introduction to the person and ministry of the Holy Spirit. Matt draws our attention to how indispensable the Holy Spirit is to every aspect of the Christian life. And while Christians more naturally relate to the Father or Jesus, Matt's book will help us appreciate, interact with, and rely on the Holy Spirit both in our ministries and our personal lives.

Michael Brown
President at AskDrBrownMinistries and
author of *Israel's Divine Healer*

THE HOLY SPIRIT

An Introduction

THE HOLY SPIRIT

An Introduction

MATT AYARS

Copyright 2023 by Matthew I. Ayars

All rights reserved. No part of this publication may be reproduced, stored in a retrieval system, or transmitted, in any form or by any means—electronic, mechanical, photocopying, recording, or otherwise—without prior written permission, except for brief quotations in critical reviews or articles.

Unless otherwise noted Scripture quotations are from the ESV® Bible (The Holy Bible, English Standard Version®), copyright © 2001 by Crossway, a publishing ministry of Good News Publishers. Used by permission. All rights reserved.

Scripture quotations marked NRSVCE are from the Catholic Edition of the New Revised Standard Version Bible: Catholic Edition, copyright © 1989, 1993 National Council of the Churches of Christ in the United States of America. Used by permission. All rights reserved worldwide.

Scripture quotations marked NASB taken from the New American Standard Bible® (NASB), Copyright © 1960, 1962, 1963, 1968, 1971, 1972, 1973, 1975, 1977, 1995 by The Lockman Foundation. Used by permission. www.Lockman.org.

Scripture quotations marked KJV are taken from the Holy Bible, King James Version, Cambridge, 1796.

Printed in the United States of America

Cover design and layout by Strange Last Name
Page design and layout by PerfecType, Nashville, Tennessee

Ayars, Matthew I.
　The Holy Spirit : an introduction / Matt Ayars. – Franklin, Tennessee : Seedbed Publishing, ©2023.

　　　pages ; cm.

　　　Includes bibliographical references and index.
　　　ISBN: 9781628249989 (paperback)
　　　ISBN: 9781628249996 (mobi)
　　　ISBN: 9798888000007 (epub)
　　　ISBN: 9798888000014 (pdf)
　　　OCLC: 1376008092

　　　1. Holy Spirit.　I. Title.

BT121.3 A92 2023　　　　　　　　　　　　231.3　　　　2023936163

SEEDBED PUBLISHING
Franklin, Tennessee
Seedbed.com

CONTENTS

Acknowledgments — xi
Introduction: Holiness, the Holy Spirit, and the Glory of God — 1

Chapter 1: The Bible as the Primary Source — 17
Chapter 2: Church Tradition and Doctrine — 35

Part I: The Identity of the Holy Spirit

Chapter 3: The Holy Spirit within the Trinity — 47
Chapter 4: The Holy Spirit Is God — 67
Chapter 5: The Holy Spirit Is a Person — 85

Part II: The Ministry of the Holy Spirit

Chapter 6: The Holy Spirit and Salvation — 97
Chapter 7: The Holy Spirit and the Church — 157

Chapter 8: The Holy Spirit and End Times	183
Chapter 9: The Holy Spirit and the Holy Life	193
Conclusion	205
Bibliography	209
Scripture Index	219

ACKNOWLEDGMENTS

I am indebted to an entire network of friends and colleagues for their help in developing this book. First and foremost, my former professor, dear friend, and colleague Dr. Steve Blakemore has helped me beyond all others. His theological knowledge is not as one who gazes upon the Trinity from afar, but as one who has shared in the interior life of God through union with Christ in the Holy Spirit.

I'm also indebted to Dr. Chris Lohrstorfer for helping me strengthen my grasp on some of the distinctives of Wesleyan-Arminian pneumatology and soteriology. Dr. Lohrstorfer takes the back seat to no one (at least that I know of) when it comes to knowledge of Wesley's theology.

Finally, special thanks go to Dr. Tom McCall, who is always a gracious and constant source of encouragement and stimulating dialogue. Being able to draw on him and his grasp on the broader landscape and current state of theological studies proved invaluable to me in this project from start to finish.

I can say with utmost confidence any mistakes or imperfections in the pages that follow are entirely my own.

The use of the term "God" here always assumes the philosophical predicate "triune." References to specific persons of the Trinity will be explicitly stated. Lastly, following the example of the Scriptures, I refer to the Holy Spirit with masculine pronouns (John 14:17, 26; Romans 8:11, 16).

INTRODUCTION

Holiness, the Holy Spirit, and the Glory of God

In the early verses of Exodus 3, Moses is keeping his father-in-law's sheep at the foot of Mount Sinai when he sees something strange. He sees a bush engulfed in flames, but the fire is not consuming it. As Moses approaches to get a better look at the peculiar sight, God speaks to him out of the flames in the heart of the bush. God tells Moses that if he comes any closer, he must remove his sandals because the ground on which he is standing is holy (Ex. 3:5). In other words, this ground is no ordinary ground. This ground is *different* because God's personal presence is there in the heart of the bush.

This story contains the seed of a central theme that is unpacked in high-resolution detail through the rest of the Bible: God's holiness. The holiness of God is at the center of who God reveals himself to be in Scripture. God's holiness is the most important thing about him. Yes, God is all-powerful, faithful, and incorruptibly good, but even before all of that, he is *holy*. The top priority of the holiness of God in Scripture is why holiness is the most appropriate starting point for a study of the Holy Spirit. Just like Moses, if we want to take a step closer to knowing God—and in this case, God the Holy Spirit—we must first come to grips with his holiness.

Holiness: A Definition

So, what does it mean that God is holy? The word *holy*, in the most basic sense, means "different." First Samuel 2:2 captures this well. It says: "There is none holy like the Lord: for there is none besides you; there is no rock like our God." So, when we say that God is holy, we mean that God is *different*.

I Am: The Transcendence of God

How is God different? A few verses after God tells Moses to remove his sandals, he tells Moses that his name is "I Am" (Ex. 3:14). What does this mean? For starters, God is saying that unlike created beings, he is entirely *independent* and *unlimited*. In a word, God is *transcendent*. Like all created beings, human beings are utterly dependent on creation for their existence. We are also bound by time and space. We cannot be in more than one place at once. God can. People cannot be in the past, present, and future all at once. God can. Every created being has a beginning. God doesn't. Humans are a part of creation, and creation is a part of them. We are continuous with the creation. God is not. God is not dependent on the creation and not limited by time or space because God is not a created being, unlike everything else. God simply *is*. God's unique existence in the category of "uncreated being" makes him *different* from everything else in the creation.

No Idolatry: It's Too Small

The transcendence and eternality of God are the reasons behind the Bible's strong prohibitions against making idols. God is so wholly other than the creation that nothing within it can contain him. Trying to fit God into a statue would be like trying to fit the Pacific Ocean in a teacup. The teacup cannot even come close to containing all the water of the ocean. Likewise, no created thing can come remotely close to containing God or representing him adequately. God is always more than anything shaped by human hands because he has no limits. All created things and beings fall infinitely short of fully describing him. Trying to fit God into something that is created would diminish him and thereby be a false representation of who he is. Idolatry,

> God's unique existence in the category of "uncreated being" makes him different from everything else in the creation.... Idolatry, by necessity, diminishes the triune God to something that he is not.

by necessity, diminishes the triune God to something that he is not.

But why is it such a big deal that people do not make idols? The problem with idolatry is not that a statue cannot contain God. The real problem is that idols *misrepresent* him. The prohibition against idolatry tells us that it is of critical importance that people understand that God is holy, different. God prohibits people from making idols because it's important to him that people know him properly and don't have the wrong idea of who he is. Anything less than the I Am is an imposter.

The Knowability of God

These concepts can be challenging to grasp. The idea that God is not restricted by time and space and is without limits is so different from human reality that we can't fully understand it. It's challenging to think about even by the greatest stretch of the imagination. In short, it's a mystery.

> Our goal is not just to learn about God the Holy Spirit but also to know him personally.

What does this have to do with the Holy Spirit? For starters, because God is so other than anything we can comprehend, we need someone to help us understand him. We need a helper to interpret God to our minds and hearts. The Holy Spirit is that Helper. A fruitful study of God requires assistance from the Holy Spirit. Just as the Holy Spirit helps us understand the Bible, he helps us know God. Only the Holy Spirit has the ability, as God, to bring a knowledge of God to us and to help us know him personally. Our goal is not just to learn about God the Holy Spirit but also to know him personally. One of the ways he does that is by pointing us to Jesus.

Jesus as Divine Revelation

The Old Testament tells us that God reveals himself in both the creation and the Bible (Ps. 19). The New Testament affirms that teaching but adds that Jesus himself is the most accurate, excellent, and foremost form of divine revelation because he is the very incarnation of God. Hebrews 1:1–4 says:

> Long ago, at many times and in many ways, God spoke to our fathers by the prophets, but in these last days he has spoken to us by his Son, whom he appointed the heir of all things, through whom also he created the world. He is the radiance of the glory of God and the exact imprint of his nature, and he upholds the universe by the word of his power. After making purification for sins, he

The New Testament tells us that if we want to know what God looks like, look to Jesus. If you want to know God personally, know Jesus.

sat down at the right hand of the Majesty on high, having become as much superior to angels as the name he has inherited is more excellent than theirs.

In other words, Jesus, more than the creation and the Scriptures themselves, reveals God. The New Testament tells us that if we want to know what God looks like, look to Jesus (John 14:9). If you want to know God personally, know Jesus. While nothing in the creation can truly embody God, Jesus can and does.

Paul says this about Jesus:

He is the image of the invisible God, the firstborn of all creation. For by him all things were created, in heaven and on earth, visible and invisible, whether thrones or dominions or rulers or authorities—all things were created through him and for him. And he is before all things, and in him all things hold together. And he is the head of the body, the church. He is the beginning, the firstborn from the dead, that in everything he might be preeminent. For in him all the fullness of God was pleased to dwell, and through him to reconcile to himself all things, whether on earth or in heaven, making peace by the blood of his cross. (Col. 1:15–20, italics added)

Did you catch that? If you want to see God, look at Jesus.

When You're with Jesus, You're with God

Mark 2 tells of a paralyzed man taken to Jesus for healing. When Jesus sees the man, he says, "Your sins are forgiven." The Bible then tells us that there were Pharisees present who didn't like that Jesus forgave the man's sins because only God can forgive sins. They didn't understand that Jesus is God. Usually, you would have to go to the temple to get your sins forgiven because that's where God's presence was. When Jesus forgave this man's sins, he was saying that when you're with him, you're with God, just as if you were at the temple.

> By equating Jesus with the temple of God, John's telling us that Jesus is God. Jesus is the place where heaven and earth meet.

The story of Jesus driving the money changers and vendors from the temple in John 2 has a similar point. After driving the vendors out of the temple, the priests question Jesus's authority to do this. Jesus responded by saying that the sign of his authority was that he would destroy the temple and, in three days, rebuild it. John goes on to say that Jesus was talking about the temple of his body (John 2:21). By equating Jesus with the temple of God, John's telling us that Jesus is God. Jesus is the place where heaven and earth meet.

Most explicitly, John says, "In the beginning was the Word, and the Word was with God, *and the Word was God*" (John 1:1, italics added). He goes on to say a few verses later:

"And the Word became flesh and dwelt among us, and we have seen his glory, glory as of the only Son from the Father, full of grace and truth" (John 1:14). Once again, John is saying that Jesus is God. Jesus himself says in John 14:9, "Whoever has seen me has seen the Father." So, while God is entirely different than anything created, Jesus makes God known as the very embodiment of God.

Revelation and Personal Relationship

There is a big difference between knowing about someone and knowing someone personally. Anyone can read a biography of George Washington and learn all sorts of facts about his life. You can learn about his upbringing, education, parents, where he lived, passions and hobbies, accomplishments, and failures. However, knowing *about* George Washington does not mean that you *know him personally*. When you learn about someone, it may feel as if you know them personally (which is why we have a sense of personal attachment to the people we know so much about). Still, ultimately you only know about them because for you to know someone personally, they must know you too. There is a reciprocal nature to knowing someone personally. Personal relationships consist of both giving and receiving.

Being in a relationship with someone means to know and to be known.

What makes Jesus the unique, preeminent revelation of God is that because he is a person (not the creation or a book), he makes it possible for people to know God personally. Jesus makes it possible for individuals to be in a personal relationship with the holy, triune God. As we will see in later chapters, the Holy Spirit unifies believers with Christ, which means that by the Holy Spirit, we can be in a giving and receiving relationship within the very life of the Trinity. In other words, the Holy Spirit—based on Christ's redeeming work—makes it possible for us to participate in the holy life of God.

> In other words, the Holy Spirit—based on Christ's redeeming work—makes it possible for us to participate in the holy life of God.

The Holy Spirit Glorifies Jesus

But where does the Holy Spirit fit into the broader picture of God's holiness and Jesus as special revelation? In John 16:14, Jesus says, "He [the Holy Spirit] will glorify me, for he will take what is mine and declare it to you." Among the many things the Holy Spirit accomplishes, one of the main things is to glorify Jesus. This means that when we study the Holy Spirit, we will find him pointing us to Jesus, just like Jesus points us to the Father. Jesus is the portrait of God, and the

Holy Spirit is the spotlight on the portrait. The Holy Spirit is self-effacing, meaning that he doesn't claim attention for himself. He is other-oriented. He is always pointing to the other two persons of the Trinity, which is why we can't talk about God the Holy Spirit without talking about God the Son and God the Father with him. As soon as you start talking about the Holy Spirit, no sooner than you know it, you're talking about the Father and the Son as well.

> As soon as you start talking about the Holy Spirit, no sooner than you know it, you're talking about the Father and the Son as well.

How does all this impact the study of the Holy Spirit? It means that the Holy Spirit, as the Helper, is not interested in helping people simply know about God. He wants us to know God personally by enabling fellowship with Jesus for the sake of a radical transformation of our very nature.

Holiness and the Character of God: Holy Love

God is other in his transcendence, but he is also other in his moral character. God is entirely good and incorruptible, unlike the creation (and humanity, in particular). He is free from any wickedness or evil. God is perfectly truthful, merciful, loving, kind, just, and righteous. In a phrase, God is perfect, *holy love* (1 John 4:7–21). This is a love that is not lacking or deficient in any way. It is the love that the holy Trinity shared in eternity before the creation. It is the same love that inspired Jesus's perfect obedience and his self-sacrifice for his enemies. It is a life-giving love that brings people back from the dead.

But what does the goodness of God have to do with the Holy Spirit? Everything. One of this book's central aims is to paint a picture of how this perfect, holy love of God takes up residence in the human heart through the Holy Spirit. The cure of the problem of the human condition is the indwelling, personal presence ("Presence,"[1] henceforth) of God through the Holy Spirit. The point of the cross is to restore God's personal Presence that was lost in the garden of Eden. Jesus ascends to heaven to restore the divine Presence to all people by sending the Holy Spirit into the human heart. When the Spirit takes up residence in our hearts, God's very Presence, marked by his holy love, fills us. When the Holy Spirit fills us, the perfect

> The cure of the problem of the human condition is the indwelling, personal presence of God through the Holy Spirit.

---

[1]. For the remainder of the book, "Presence" (capitalized) will refer to the personal presence of God, which is distinct from the general way in which God's presence is everywhere in the creation (omnipresence).

love of God that is shared between the Father, the Son, and the Holy Spirit is extended to you and me. And, when we are filled with the perfect love of God, and the Spirit breaks the power of canceled sin and even uproots the sin that corrupts our very nature, God is glorified in the world. Therefore, the aim of this study is for people to know the personal Presence of God in the Holy Spirit for the glory of God.

Overview of the Study

In arriving at a personal knowledge of the Holy Spirit, we look to the Scriptures to learn what the triune God has revealed about the Holy Spirit. We rely on the Bible as divine revelation that is inspired, inerrant, unified, sufficient, and clear for an accurate picture of the Holy Spirit and language for describing him. As we said before, nothing within the creation is an adequate container or representation of God. This includes human language. However, the Bible, as the inspired Word of God, gives us God's authorized language for describing him accurately. We also look to the creeds and councils of early Christianity to learn from the faithful ones who have gone before us. The creeds and the councils provide insight into

> The aim of this study is for people to know the personal Presence of God in the Holy Spirit for the glory of God.

how the early church interpreted the Scriptures and their experience with the Holy Spirit. We will see that the creeds and councils of the earliest Christians are not human invention, but Holy Spirit–inspired language for preserving the apostolic witness of the New Testament in the face of emerging challenges they faced together as a church. The first chapter defines this study's convictions about the Bible as the primary source for reliable teaching on the Holy Spirit. Chapter 2 explains the place and reliability of doctrine from church tradition.

After that, we will ask and answer questions about the identity of the Holy Spirit. We will find that the Scriptures reveal that the Holy Spirit is a divine person who is coequal, coeternal, and indivisibly united with God the Father and God the Son. We will explore how the Holy Spirit, while sharing the same divine essence with the other two persons of the Trinity, is distinct from the Father and the Son in that he eternally proceeds from the Father (and the Son). We will also examine why this teaching is essential by considering what is lost if we deny or reject the Bible's clear teaching and the church's universal affirmation that the Holy Spirit is a divine person.

After looking at the identity of the Holy Spirit, we will consider the ministry of the Holy Spirit. In sum, we will see

> The Holy Spirit, while sharing the same divine essence with the other two persons of the Trinity, is distinct from the Father and the Son.

that the Holy Spirit redeems God's original plans for humans and the creation by restoring the divine-human relationship on the merits of Christ's saving work. We will find that the problem of the human condition is the loss of a personal relationship with God resulting from human rebellion. We will consider how someone is saved (i.e., the way of salvation) and the role of the Holy Spirit in each stage of that process. From the softening of the heart to conviction, repentance, regeneration, justifying faith, forgiveness, inner transformation, and finally resurrection, the Holy Spirit is the key actor in restoring the image of God in humanity for the glory of God.

> The Holy Spirit is the key actor in restoring the image of God in humanity for the glory of God.

To conclude the study, we will explore how the ministry of the Holy Spirit relates to what the Bible teaches about the church, as well as end times. We will see that the Holy Spirit births, sustains, comforts, and empowers the church as the collective body of Christ-followers while we await Christ's triumphant return. We will also see that one of the purposes of sanctification by the Holy Spirit is to mark those who will be saved in the final judgment. He will vindicate (i.e., publicly prove righteous) Christians as God's people in the end times through bodily resurrection just as he did for Jesus.

Ultimately, taking all the pieces together as a whole, the Holy Spirit glorifies God the Father and God the Son by restoring the image of God in people on the merits of Jesus's life, death, and resurrection. The Holy Spirit makes the good, faithful, life-giving, and loving God visible in the world by magnifying Jesus through his faithful followers.

Questions for Reflection or Discussion

1. What is the meaning of "holy"?
2. What are the two ways in which God is set apart, or different, from created beings?
3. God is incomprehensible, yet we can know about him and have a personal relationship with him. How is that possible?
4. What is the difference between general revelation and special revelation?
5. How does the Holy Spirit glorify Jesus?

CHAPTER 1

The Bible as the Primary Source

We said in the introduction that the Bible is the primary source for our study of the Holy Spirit. This means that the Bible is our source for understanding how we can know about the Holy Spirit and know the Holy Spirit personally. Before jumping right into what the Bible says about the Holy Spirit, I will lay out my assumptions and convictions about the Bible. In this chapter, we will cover the classical Christian doctrine of bibliology, which is the Christian teaching and understanding of the Bible as the Word of God. This is particularly important for a study on the Holy Spirit because—as we will see in later chapters—the Holy Spirit has a key role in the writing and interpretation of the Bible. This section, then, will not only explore classical Christian bibliology, but particularly the relationship between the view of Scripture and the Holy Spirit's revealing work. In the sections that follow we will consider the following aspects of the Scriptures as they relate to the study of the Holy Spirit:

- the uniqueness of the Christian Bible as divine revelation
- the inspiration and authority of Scripture
- the infallibility of Scripture
- the sufficiency of Scripture
- the clarity of Scripture
- the unity of Scripture

The Bible as the Community Witness of God's Revelation

Standing in the broader currents of the great Christian tradition, the cornerstone principle of my view of the Scriptures is that the Bible is what it claims to be. In other words, I believe that the Bible's claims about itself are valid. Thus, when 2 Timothy 3:16–17 says that "All Scripture is breathed out by God and profitable for teaching, for reproof, for correction, and for training in righteousness, that the man of God may be complete, equipped for every good work," I take it at face value.

But why do I take the Bible's claim about itself at face value? The Qur'an also claims that it is the word of God, but we don't take that claim at face value. What makes the Bible unique in that sense?

The short answer is the ressurection of Jesus. Jesus, who was declared to be the

> Jesus, who was declared to be the Son of God in his resurrection, endorses the Old Testament.

Son of God in his resurrection, endorses the Old Testament. That Jesus alone was raised from the dead to a glorified body means that he is in a category of his own regarding authoritative and reliable teaching. Jesus's other miracles also validate this claim. The Spirit-led conviction of the church has always been to follow the man who healed people, calmed storms, walked on water, cast out demons, brought people back to life, and was resurrected after being dead for three days. There has never been anyone like that in history. Jesus, being in a category of his own, affirmed the Old Testament as Scripture (Matt. 5:12; 21:42; 22:29; 26:54; Luke 24:27; John 10:35). If he says it is Scripture, then it must be.

But what about the New Testament? The New Testament is the account of firsthand witnesses to Jesus. Church history attests to several criteria for determining which writings made it into the New Testament as Christian scripture. First, scripture (writings inspired by the Holy Spirit for the whole church) is always evidenced in its ability to transform readers. In other words, there is a particular self-authenticating quality to Holy Spirit–inspired writing that sets it apart from ordinary writings. A second criterion for determining canonicity was used in Christian worship. Certain books were commonly used by the earliest Christ-followers, and those books—the church decided—should be a part of the Christian Scriptures. The third and most essential factor in determining a book's inclusion into the New Testament is apostolicity; that is, a direct connection to someone who knew Jesus firsthand. For a text to be considered as divinely inspired, its author had to have proximity to either Jesus himself or one degree of separation from Jesus via an apostle. If there was any doubt over an author's direct connection to an apostle, the early church did not accept that author's text as divinely inspired. There has been consensus that the New Testament contained twenty-seven books beginning at the end of the apostolic era. In other words, even though the criteria for New Testament canonicity was not firmly declared until the fourth century AD, the recognition of the twenty-seven books of the New Testament as we have it today originated immediately following Jesus.

The second thing that makes the Bible unique is that it is the Word of God according to the witness of a community. One man in a cave wrote the Qur'an.[1] Multiple individuals wrote the Bible over time, and its claims were affirmed and verified by a community of firsthand witnesses. When God revealed himself in real time and space in word and deed, it was in the presence of a community of individuals who uphold the witness of the truthfulness of the Bible's claims. The witness of the community is what makes the Bible unique and trustworthy. This communal

> When the Bible says that it is the Word of God, then we believe it because it has the backing of historical witnesses.

---

1. The authorship of the Qur'an is more complicated than this, but the common view is that Muhammed alone is the originator of the written text.

witness is true for both the Old and New Testaments. Thus, when the Bible says that it is the Word of God, then we believe it because it has the backing of historical witnesses.

How does the uniqueness of Scripture relate to the Holy Spirit? First, Jesus, the risen one, had a lot to say about the Holy Spirit. The risen one is a reliable source. What Jesus tells us about the Holy Spirit we know to be reliable because he was vindicated as the divine Son of God in his resurrection. Related to this same dynamic, we know that the Old Testament's teaching on the Holy Spirit is trustworthy and reliable because Jesus endorsed the divine inspiration of the Old Testament. Second, what the Bible says about the Holy Spirit is what God revealed to a community of witnesses in real time and space. There were individuals and groups who stood by the claims of Scripture and what they said about the Holy Spirit. In other words, what the Scriptures say regarding the person and work of the Holy Spirit is affirmed by firsthand witnesses as trustworthy.

> What Jesus tells us about the Holy Spirit we know to be reliable because he was vindicated as the divine Son of God in his resurrection.

The Inspiration and Authority of Scripture

The most important claim that the Bible makes about itself is that God inspired it. Once again, 2 Timothy 3:16–17 says: "All Scripture is breathed out by God and profitable for teaching, for reproof, for correction, and for training in righteousness, that the man of God may be complete, equipped for every good work."[2] This means that the Bible is God-breathed, a metaphor that the Bible is *from* God; God is the source or origin of his self-revelation in the Scriptures. The Bible is not merely a human accounting of the witness of God's redemptive work in history. Rather, the Bible is God's inspiration of human authors to write the story the way he wanted it written (2 Peter 1:20–21).

That God is the source and originator of the Bible implies its authority. It carries the very authority of God in itself. As the holy, infinite Creator, God has the power and is entitled to give orders, and the Bible carries that same power and entitlement. Isaiah 45:9–12 says:

> "Woe to him who strives with him who formed him,
> > a pot among earthen pots!
> Does the clay say to him who forms it, 'What are you making?'
> > or 'Your work has no handles'?
> Woe to him who says to a father, 'What are you begetting?'
> > or to a woman, 'With what are you in labor?'"

---

2. See also Nehemiah 9:30; Matthew 22:43–44; 1 Corinthians 2:13; 2 Peter 1:20–21; Hebrews 1:1–2.

Thus says the LORD,
> the Holy One of Israel, and the one who formed him:
"Ask me of things to come;
> will you command me concerning my children
> and the work of my hands?
I made the earth
> and created man on it;
it was my hands that stretched out the heavens,
> and I commanded all their host."

Because God is the source of all things (including human life), he alone has the right and privilege to give commands; because God is the source of the Holy Scriptures, the Bible itself has authority. Disobeying the Bible is the same as disobeying God himself.

The doctrine of the inspiration of Scripture is also why Christians believe that the Bible is a living document. Hebrews 4:12–13 says: "For the word of God is living and active, sharper than any two-edged sword, piercing to the division of soul and of spirit, of joints and of marrow, and discerning the thoughts and intentions of the heart. And no creature is

> "For the word of God is living and active, sharper than any two-edged sword, piercing to the division of soul and of spirit, of joints and of marrow, and discerning the thoughts and intentions of the heart."

hidden from his sight, but all are naked and exposed to the eyes of him to whom we must give account."

The Word of God is alive because God breathes life into the Word, as well as into believers who read the Word to love and obey God. As we will explore in detail in later chapters, the Holy Spirit is always associated with the life-giving activity of God. When we say that God breathes life into something (e.g., the Word) or someone, it is God the Holy Spirit who gives life. With this, we can say that God inspires the writing of the Word, and that God inspires the interpretation of the Word.

> The Word of God is alive because God breathes life into the Word, as well as into believers who read the Word to love and obey God.

What does the inspiration and authority of Scripture have to do with the Holy Spirit? First, it means that what the Bible reveals about the Holy Spirit comes from the Holy Spirit himself, since the Spirit played an integral role in the writing of the Word of God. Second, what the Bible says about the Holy Spirit is authoritative, meaning that challenging what the Bible says about the Holy Spirit is the same as challenging God himself on the matter. Those whose teachings on the Holy Spirit deviate from the Scriptures are dangerous because they contradict what God himself says on the subject. Third, the inspiration of the Scriptures means that since the Holy Spirit was instrumental in the writing of the Word, then he is also instrumental in the interpretation of the Word. As we will explore in more detail in the sections on the clarity of Scripture and the role of Christian tradition, the Holy Spirit helps us interpret the deeper theological meaning of the Bible when we read it seeking to love and obey God.

The Infallibility of Scripture

The doctrine of the infallibility of Scripture is in some ways very straightforward, and in other ways rather complicated. The doctrine simply stated is that *the Bible is entirely trustworthy in its teaching*. In other words, the Bible does not contain any falsehoods or lead readers astray. It is entirely reliable as God's self-revelation. Alan Cairns offers a more robust definition of infallibility:

> That quality of the Bible, the inspired word of God, by which it is free from error, authentic in its writings, reliable in its revelation, and authoritative in all its communications. In other words, infallibility means that the Scripture, whether considered in its totality or in any of its

> The doctrine of infallability simply stated is that *the Bible is entirely trustworthy in its teaching.*

parts cannot fall short of being true, whatever the subject under consideration may be.[3]

This doctrine is the natural result of the doctrine of inspiration. It affirms that when God reveals himself in Scripture, he does so without fault or error. If the Bible is inspired by God (meaning that God is the source of the Bible) and God (1) knows all things (Ps. 147:5; 1 John 3:20) and (2) does not lie (Tit. 1:2), then a falsehood in Scripture means that God is either lying or limited in his knowledge, both of which the Scriptures refute. Let's unpack this a bit more.

> Infallability is the natural result of the doctrine of inspiration. It affirms that when God reveals himself in Scripture, he does so without fault or error.

First, the Bible clearly says that God knows all things (i.e., God is omniscient). Scripture tells us that God's understanding is beyond measure (Ps. 147:5), that he knows everything (1 John 3:20), that the hairs of every human head and the stars are numbered (Matt. 10:30; Ps. 147:4), and that no creature is hidden from God's sight and that all things are laid bare to God's eyes (Heb. 4:13). In short, God is omniscient, meaning

---

3. Alan Cairns, *Dictionary of Theological Terms: A Ready Reference of Over 800 Theological and Doctrinal Terms* (Greenville, SC: Ambassador Emerald International, 2002), 232.

"all-knowing." There is nothing that God does not know or understand.

Second, the Bible also definitively declares that God does not lie (Num. 23:19; Titus 1:2). Hebrews 6:18 says: "so that by two unchangeable things, *in which it is impossible for God to lie*, we who have fled for refuge might have strong encouragement to hold fast to the hope set before us" (italics added). God is honest, true, and reliable.

What do God's omniscience and honesty have to do with the Bible being trustworthy? If the Bible contains falsehoods, then God either (1) doesn't know any better or (2) is giving misinformation (i.e., lying). Put another way, if God knows everything, then to declare a falsehood would be a lie or misleading. Likewise, if God does not lie yet states a falsehood, he is not all-knowing. To suggest that the Bible affirms things that are not true implies that God is either limited in knowledge or not trustworthy, both of which the Bible refutes.

> It is precisely because the Holy Spirit played an active role in creating the Bible that it is trustworthy and reliable.

One of the significant dangers of rejecting the infallibility of Scripture is that to do so makes the Bible an inferior standard for measuring truth. It diminishes the reliability of Scripture. To make the Bible inferior to anything else such as science or human reason as a standard for measuring truth is to undermine God's supremacy, sovereignty, authority, and truthfulness—all of which directly contradicts the very commands of Scripture. To reject the infallability of Scripture is to reject God as he has revealed himself in the Bible, or to reject inspiration.

What does the doctrine of the infallibility of Scripture have to do with the Holy Spirit? First, *it is precisely because the Holy Spirit played an active role in creating the Bible that it is trustworthy and reliable*. Because the Holy Spirit is God, we can fully and without hesitation or reserve trust what he inspired the human authors of Scripture to write. Second, what the Bible says about the Holy Spirit is trustworthy and reliable. The Bible does not mislead readers about who the Holy Spirit is or what he does in the world.

> The doctrine of the sufficiency of Scripture says that the Bible contains everything necessary for people to live a life that is wholly pleasing to God.

The Sufficiency of Scripture

The doctrine of the sufficiency of Scripture says that the Bible contains everything necessary for people to live a life that is wholly pleasing to God (Pss. 1, 19, and 119). Nothing is missing from Scripture and nothing needs to be added to Scripture to live in complete obedience to God. The curses against those who take away from or add to the Scriptures are the foundations for the doctrine. Revelation 22:18–19 says: "I warn everyone who hears the words of the prophecy of this book: if anyone adds to them, God will add to him the plagues described in this book, and if anyone takes away from the words of the book of this prophecy, God will take away his share in the tree of life and in the holy city, which are described in this book." This strong warning is because, on the one hand, taking away from the Scriptures means preventing people from living a life that is fully pleasing to God. On the other hand, adding to the Scriptures requires more of people than what God himself requires for righteousness.

The sufficiency of Scripture as special revelation is in contrast with the insufficiency of general revelation. While we can know about God through nature and our internal moral compass, nature and the moral conscience cannot bring us to a *personal relationship* with God. The Bible, however, is sufficient for a personal relationship with God.

> The doctrine of the clarity of Scripture states that the Holy Spirit clarifies the text's message to those who read it with a desire to love and obey God.

The impact of the sufficiency of Scripture on the study of the Holy Spirit is that the Scriptures contain everything that we need to know about the Holy Spirit to be saved. There is not something about the Holy Spirit missing from the Scriptures that we need human teaching or experience to supplement. Everything that God has ordained for people to know about the Holy Spirit can be found in the Bible.

The Clarity of Scripture

Psalm 19:7 says: "The law of the Lord is perfect, reviving the soul; the testimony of the Lord is sure, making wise the simple." This means that even the simple can understand the Bible. Furthermore, the Bible commands believers to teach their children the Scriptures (Deut. 6:7). If the Bible can make wise the simple and even children can understand it, then the text's message must be clear and comprehensible. More precisely, the doctrine of the clarity of Scripture states that the Holy Spirit clarifies the text's message to those who read it with a desire to love and obey God.

> While there is a sense of divine mystery to the Holy Spirit, the Bible tells readers what they need to know about him and how to know about him and to know him personally.

The first thing to highlight here is the role of the Holy Spirit. The Holy Spirit inspired both the writing of the text and the reading of the text. The Holy Spirit interprets the meaning of the Word to our hearts and helps us accept the Word as good and true. As we will explore in later chapters, faith is a gift of the Holy Spirit, meaning that the Holy Spirit helps readers understand, believe, and obey the Word.

The clarity of Scripture tells us that what the Bible says about the Holy Spirit is understandable and accessible. The

Bible reveals that the Holy Spirit is not hidden nor incomprehensible. While there is a sense of divine mystery to the Holy Spirit, the Bible tells readers what they need to know about him and how to know about him and to know him personally. What the Bible says about the Holy Spirit is plain and clear.

The Unity of Scripture

If God is the source of the Bible, then the Bible must reflect God's single, comprehensive, unified mind (Deut. 6:4). The Bible does not contradict itself because God does not contradict himself. The Bible, like its source, is consistent and has an internal coherence. Additionally, since the Bible is trustworthy, reliable, and infallible it must also be unified in its message. The unity of the Bible is why we use Scripture to interpret Scripture. The meaning of specific parts of the text is derived from the whole and the whole by the parts.

> The Bible, like its divine source, is consistent and has an internal coherence.

Because the Bible is unified in its message, what the Bible reveals about the Holy Spirit will not be contradictory. For example, it will not say in the Old Testament that the Holy Spirit is not God, yet in the New Testament, say that he is God, since the entire Bible comes from God who is one.

Conclusion

The Bible is the primary source for this study of the Holy Spirit. What the Bible says about the Holy Spirit is revealed by God himself and, therefore, authoritative. Furthermore, what we learn about the Holy Spirit in Scripture is trustworthy, understandable, coherent, and sufficient for a saving relationship with God.

Why It Matters

Why does it matter that we clearly understand what we believe about the Scriptures? It's important because the Bible says that the Deceiver is like a roaring lion who roams about, seeking to devour us (1 Peter 5:8). He is a liar who wants to lead us astray through deception. The proper defense against the enemy is a clear understanding of the truth, which the Bible gives us. If the Bible contains falsehoods, we are vulnerable to being led astray. It matters that the message of the Bible is clear and sufficient for understanding salvation—and particularly for this book—the Holy Spirit. If the message of Scripture is not clear, adequate, or trustworthy, then we would lack what we need to know about the Holy Spirit and to know him personally. The clarity and sufficiency of Scripture means that we can know everything we need to know about the Holy Spirit right from the Scriptures, and this is required for living fully into the life that Jesus is offering us.

Questions for Reflection and Discussion

1. What role does the Holy Spirit play in the shaping of Scripture?
2. What is the doctrine of the infallibility of Scripture?
3. What does it mean that the Scriptures are "God-breathed"?
4. What are some of the dangers of believing that the Scriptures contain falsehoods?
5. Considering the doctrine of the clarity and simplicity of Scripture, what can we conclude if people disagree on the message and meaning of the text?

CHAPTER 2

Church Tradition and Doctrine

In the previous chapter, we said that the Bible is the foundational and authoritative source for learning about the person and work of the Holy Spirit. In this chapter, we will look at the consensual tradition of the church represented in the ancient councils and the recognized orthodox theological interpreters of the faith across the centuries as a secondary source for learning about the person and work of the Holy Spirit. We will further explore an idea from chapter 1: the Holy Spirit not only inspired the writing of the Bible, but *he also inspires the reading and interpretation of the Bible*, which is the basis for church tradition, which is better called the "Great Tradition" that is the shared lineage of all Christians.

The Need for Tradition: Interpreting the Bible

Many Christians are uneasy about the idea of church tradition as an authoritative source for an accurate understanding of God and worship. If the Bible is the inspired Word of God and sufficient for salvation, why do we need church tradition and creeds? Does following church tradition not violate the Bible's commands to not add to the Scriptures (Deut. 4:2 and Rev. 18–19)?

The answer to the objection to tradition is relatively simple: we need church tradition because the Bible—as a text—*requires interpretation*. Take, for example, the command to remember the Sabbath to keep it holy (Ex. 20:8–11). Can we wash dishes on the Sabbath? Go for a walk? Can we get out of bed? Go to the grocery store? Watch sports? Play with the kids? The point is that the command to rest on the Sabbath needs to be interpreted. Even further, it is only based on the church's theological tradition that we understand why Sunday, rather than the Sabbath, became the Christian holy day. As one theologian once said, the Bible sometimes gives us all the ingredients but doesn't always tell us how to bake the cake.

> Tradition results from moving beyond what a text *says* and arriving at what it *means*.

Tradition results from moving beyond what a text *says* and arriving at what it *means*. Tradition is founded on the conviction that the Holy Spirit inspires both the *writing* and the *reading* of Scripture (Heb. 4:12; 2 Tim. 3:16). The Holy Spirit not only gives God's people the Word of God but also helps us to understand what it means and apply it in our times. When the worshipping community arrives at an interpretation by the guidance of the Holy Spirit, that interpretation becomes tradition. *The role of tradition, then, is not to invent teaching or add to the Scriptures, but to preserve the integrity of the original meaning of Scripture with the help of the Holy Spirit.* We are significantly aided in our efforts to understand the Holy Spirit by recognizing the Great Tradition of the church and entering into dialogue with those who came before us in the effort to live faithfully.

> The role of tradition is not to invent teaching or add to the Scriptures, but to preserve the integrity of the original meaning of Scripture with the help of the Holy Spirit.

When we rely on tradition for clarity on the Holy Spirit, we must keep in mind that we are assuming that the Holy Spirit was faithful in guiding the formulation of doctrine. When we look to tradition for teaching on the Holy Spirit, we assume that the faithful community of Christians were under the guidance of the Holy Spirit in arriving at their interpretive conclusions. Relying on the church's traditions as an authority on Christian teaching by no means replaces the Scriptures with teachings of men; instead, it believes and relies upon the faithfulness of the Holy Spirit to speak in and through the church in history. Embracing church tradition is an exercise in faith that God did not fail in guiding his people in truth in the face of false teaching through the centuries.

Scripture First (*Prima Scriptura*)

Even though the Holy Spirit still speaks in and through the church, the Scriptures alone are in a particular category of divine revelation. As we explored in the previous chapter, the Bible is the inspired, authoritative, infallible, sufficient, united Word of God. While in the category of divine revelation and affirming that the Holy Spirit still speaks to illuminate our understanding, tradition is not equivalent to the Bible in its authority. While Scripture and tradition complement one another and work together, Scripture alone (*sola scriptura*) is the primary and final authority. Scripture is in a category all by itself as authoritative divine revelation. This means that tradition must be measured against Scripture and that tradition can never add to the canon of Scripture.

> While Scripture and tradition complement one another and work together, Scripture alone is the primary and final authority.

Do We Need Creeds and Councils?

Within the first few hundred years of the church, several teachings emerged that were incongruent with the worship, convictions, and beliefs of the Spirit-filled, worshipping community. Take, for example, the heresy of the *pneumatomachi* ("spirit fighters") in the fourth and fifth centuries AD. They denied that the Holy Spirit was God and taught that the Holy Spirit was created by God the Father and God the Son. At the time of the *pneumatomachi*, the church did not have a definitive statement on the divinity of the Holy Spirit, but they knew that they worshipped him just as they worshipped Jesus as the divine Son of God. The challenge to the divinity of the Spirit caused the church to revisit the Old Testament and the teachings of Jesus and the apostles in the New Testament for clarity on the matter. The Holy Spirit then led the (whole) church in interpreting passages from Scripture that taught that he was, in fact, a divine person. The result of that process was an update to the Nicene Creed at the First Council of Constantinople, which became the definitive declaration of the church's witness to the divinity of Christ. The beliefs held by all Christians are fixed in these early councils.

> We must remember that Christianity is not just a biblical religion, it is also a historical religion.

We must remember that Christianity is not just a biblical religion, it is also a historical religion. God showed up in time and space among witnesses. The Bible is the recording of that witness. The New Testament is built on the authority of what the apostles witnessed firsthand in Jesus of Nazareth. This means that councils were not deciding what was right and wrong. They were not determining orthodoxy. Instead, the early councils of the church were working out—with the help of the Holy Spirit and using accurate and faithful language—how to describe best what they inherited from the apostolic witness and the earliest worshipping communities.

Which Creeds and Which Councils?

There have been dozens of church councils that have produced numerous creedal statements through the centuries. Are they all authoritative, or only some of them? For all Christians, the only councils that are considered authoritative for all believers are those developed with representation from the whole church. The first council of this type was the Jerusalem Council from Acts 15. That council—which was attended by leaders from *every region* of the early church—determined that Gentile Christians were not required to observe the Mosaic law of the Jews. In other words, the church had to come together to interpret the teachings of Jesus to arrive at an answer for a new problem.

> The Jerusalem Council from Acts 15 determined that Gentile Christians were not required to observe the Mosaic law of the Jews.

The key dynamic of that council is that those in attendance represented the *entire church*. Leaders from the whole church were there. Global representation is the determining factor for authority. The final decision, or decree, had to be a proclamation of the unified, collective body of Christ. Kevin Vanhoozer writes:

> Church councils are called at particular times and places where decisions about something vital to the story of redemption have to be made in order to preserve the integrity of the gospel and the unity of the church (e.g., that charge that the Son is the highest created being as refuted by the *homoousios* of the Council of Nicaea). They reflect the recognition that authority is vested in the whole church, not simply a monarchy or hierarchy. "Catholicity" means the whole congregation of the faithful.[1]

The councils that meet the criteria of representation from the entire church are:

- The First Council of Nicaea (AD 325)
- The First Council of Constantinople (AD 381)
- Council of Ephesus (AD 431)

---

1. Kevin Vanhoozer, *Biblical Authority after Babel: Retrieving the Solas in the Spirit of Mere Protestant Christianity* (Grand Rapids: Brazos Press, 2016), 135.

- Council of Chalcedon (AD 553)
- Second Council of Constantinople (AD 553)
- Third Council of Constantinople (AD 680–681)
- Second Council of Nicaea (AD 787)

The two councils that brought clarity to the Bible's witness to the Holy Spirit's work and identity are the Council of Nicaea and the Council of Constantinople. Therefore, we will draw on language from these councils in this study since these are proven reliable and authoritative as doctrines that the Holy Spirit inspired and affirmed by the witness of the entire church.

Conclusion

While the Bible is the final authority on divine revelation, we also look to tradition in assistance in understanding the Holy Spirit as revealed in Scripture. The reliability and authority of tradition is based on the need for Holy Spirit–inspired interpretation of the Bible within the worshipping community. As Christians, we believe that the Holy Spirit not only inspired the writing of the Scriptures, but also the reading of the Scriptures. The fact that the Holy Spirit is the originator of the proper interpretation of the Bible makes tradition

> We believe that the Holy Spirit not only inspired the writing of the Scriptures, but also the reading of the Scriptures.

reliable and authoritative when affirmed by the witness of the entire church.

Why It Matters

Doctrine matters because the Bible needs to be interpreted. We must go from observing what the text says to what it means. Doctrine allows us to have a clear understanding of the fundamental beliefs of the Christian faith. When heresy crops up in the church, it is vital to be able to succinctly declare, with accurate language that is faithful to the message of Scripture, how wrong teaching deviates from the experience of the church and its witness in history. Doctrine, as enshrined in the creeds and the councils, provides a historical foundation directly connected to the apostolic witness that is trustworthy and faithful to the teachings of Christ. Doctrine is a concise way to understand what Christians believe and why. It ensures that worship today is consistent with those who walked with Jesus.

Questions for Reflection and Discussion

1. What role does the Holy Spirit play in shaping church tradition and doctrine?
2. Considering the doctrines of the sufficiency and clarity of Scripture, why are doctrines, creeds, and councils necessary?

3. Why is doctrine not on the same level as Scripture when it comes to reliability of knowledge about God?
4. The Bible teaches that Jesus saves, not doctrine. Why is this important?

PART I

The Identity of the Holy Spirit

In the fourth century AD, the church officially affirmed the biblical and apostolic witness of the Holy Spirit as the third person of the Trinity. That affirmation definitively declared that the Holy Spirit eternally proceeds from the Father (and the Son); is coequal, coeternal, and indivisibly united with the Father and the Son; and shares the same divine nature as the Father and the Son. This section is an overview of the key concepts at play in shaping the church's thinking about and worship of the Holy Spirit as foundational to understanding the divinity and personhood of the Holy Spirit.

CHAPTER 3

The Holy Spirit within the Trinity

Luke 24 tells the story of two men walking to a village called Emmaus. As they were walking and discussing the tragic death of Jesus and rumors of his resurrection, the resurrected Jesus appeared to them. At first, they didn't recognize him. Luke tells us that at this moment Jesus "interpreted to them in all the Scriptures the things concerning himself" (Luke 24:27). In short, Jesus showed these two men how the Bible is all about him from beginning to end.

But what does this have to do with the Trinity? Second Timothy 3:16 tells us that the Scriptures are "breathed out by God," which is a metaphor for God the Father and God the Holy Spirit as the two-pronged source of the sacred Scriptures. Since God the Father and God the Holy Spirit are the origins of the Scriptures, and the Scriptures are ultimately all about Jesus, then the three persons of the Trinity must be other-oriented. In this case, God the Father and God the Holy Spirit glorify Jesus in the Scriptures.

As we briefly noted in the introduction, each person of the Trinity points to the other. They are other-referential. Jesus points to the Father (John 14:9) and the Spirit (John 20:22), and the Spirit to Jesus (John 14:16; 16:14) and therefore to the Father (1 Cor. 2:10), and the Father to Jesus (John 17:1) and the Spirit (Luke 11:13; Acts 5:32).

The other-oriented nature of the Trinity is why we can't study the Holy Spirit by himself. We can only truly understand the Holy Spirit as he exists in relationship to God the Father and God the Son. More specifically, we can only understand the Holy Spirit *through the Son*.[1] Nevertheless, we have to understand the Trinity to understand the Holy Spirit. The very nature of the Trinity itself is that one cannot be understood apart from the other. To understand the Holy Spirit, we have to understand the Father and the Son together with him. They are wrapped up in one another. Fourth-century theologian Gregory Nazianzus wrote: "No sooner do I conceive of the one then I am illumined by the splendor of the three; no sooner do I distinguish them than I am carried back to the one."[2] So, before jumping directly

> The very nature of the Trinity itself is that one cannot be understood apart from the other.

---

1. More on this in the section on the eternal procession of the Spirit.
2. Gregory of Nazianzus, *Oration* 40, "On Holy Baptism," 41; *NPNF2* 7:375.

into the personhood and the divinity of the Holy Spirit, let's first lay the groundwork for the fundamentals of the Trinity.

Old Testament Monotheism

One of the most important lessons about God in the Old Testament is that he is one. This is most explicitly stated in the Old Testament's definitive declaration of the oneness of God in Deuteronomy 6:4, which says: "Hear, O Israel: The LORD our God, the LORD is one." Complementing Deuteronomy 6:4 are the first two commands of the Ten Commandments: (1) you shall have no other gods before me, and (2) You shall not make for yourself a carved image (Deut. 5:7–8). The Old Testament's prohibition of high places further pressed the urgency of the unicity of God. It was imperative that Israel had only one place of worship because multiple places of worship confused the witness of the oneness of God.

> It was imperative that Israel had only one place of worship because multiple places of worship confused the witness of the oneness of God.

This was odd to Israel's neighbors. Every other people group around Israel believed in and worshipped multiple gods. They were polytheists. When God revealed himself to Israel as the one true God, it was contrary to the way everyone else understood the world. Because monotheism was unheard of, it made it all the more important that Israel's witness was faithful. In revealing himself as one, God was correcting the way the entire world got it wrong. The nation of Israel was to be the messenger to the world proclaiming that there was one God, not many, and that he was different than all the other imposter gods. God cared deeply that his creation thought rightly about him, which is why the Old Testament is so persistent on the truth of the matter: God is one.

The Divinity of Jesus

Against the backdrop of the Old Testament's persistence of the oneness of God, it is understandable why Jesus was sentenced to death for his claim that he was equal with God. His implied divinity was clear. John 8:57–59 says:

> So the Jews said to him, "You are not yet fifty years old, and have you seen Abraham?" Jesus said to them, "Truly, truly, I say to you, before Abraham was, I am." So they picked up stones to throw at him, but Jesus hid himself and went out of the temple.

When Jesus says, "before Abraham was, I am," he is referring to the divine name of God revealed in Exodus 3:14. He's saying, "Just as God is the 'I Am,' so am I." He adds, "before Abraham was," which emphasizes that Jesus is eternally preexistent. Yes, Jesus is saying that he is eternal, that he existed before he was conceived in the womb of Mary. As we will see later in this study, eternality is an attribute of God alone. If Jesus is the I Am and eternal, then he must be divine.

The Jewish scribes were also agitated when Jesus forgave the sins of a paralytic because forgiving sins is something only God has the authority to do. Mark 2:5-7 says:

> And when Jesus saw their faith, he said to the paralytic, "Son, your sins are forgiven." Now some of the scribes were sitting there, questioning in their hearts, "Why does this man speak like that? He is blaspheming! Who can forgive sins but God alone?"

When Jesus did what God alone has the authority to do, he was making himself equal with God.

Additionally, as Jesus was on trial before the Sanhedrin (the high priestly court of ancient Judaism) before being sentenced to death by Pilate, they asked him if he was the Messiah. Mark 14:62–64 says:

> Blasphemy is the act of speaking sacrilegiously about God.

> And Jesus said, "I am, and you will see the Son of Man seated at the right hand of Power and coming with the clouds of heaven." And the high priest tore his garments and said, "What further witnesses

do we need? *You have heard his blasphemy.* What is your decision?" And they all condemned him as deserving death. (italics added)

When Jesus says that he is the "Son of Man seated at the right hand of Power and coming with the clouds of heaven," he is referring to a messianic prophecy in Daniel 7, which portrays the Messiah as the divine Son of God. For Jesus to identify himself as this individual is to claim divine sonship, which is why the priests accuse Jesus of blasphemy after hearing Jesus's testimony about himself. Blasphemy is the act of speaking sacrilegiously about God. According to the priests, Jesus's claim of divine sonship is contrary to what the Old Testament teaches about the oneness of God.

From the perspective of the Pharisees, Jesus could not possibly be divine because the Old Testament clearly taught that God was *one*, not two. At the same time, Jesus's claim to be God was supported by signs and wonders, and especially his resurrection. Paul, an ardent monotheistic Jew, writes in Romans:

> Paul, a servant of Christ Jesus, called to be an apostle, set apart for the gospel of God, which he promised beforehand through his prophets in the holy Scriptures, concerning his Son, who was descended from David according to the flesh and

was declared to be the Son of God in power according to the Spirit of holiness by his resurrection from the dead, Jesus Christ our Lord. (1:1–4, italics added)[3]

By the firsthand account of the authoritative apostolic witness to the resurrection, Jesus's claims about himself were valid. He was and is the only begotten Son of God.

The early church understood this claim, which is why they worshipped Jesus just as they worshipped the God of Abraham, Isaac, and Jacob.[4] By the Holy Spirit's inspiration, the entire church unanimously understood that Jesus was not only the fulfillment of the Old Testament prophecies of a Messiah in the line of David but that, in Jesus, God joined himself to human flesh to redeem humanity.

> Jesus not only witnessed to his own divinity, he also witnessed to the divinity of the Holy Spirit, at which the Old Testament hinted.

Jesus not only witnessed to his own divinity, he also witnessed to the divinity of the Holy Spirit, at which the Old Testament hinted.[5] This is why the early church knew and understood that the apostolic witness affirmed that

---

3. See also 1 Timothy 3:16.
4. See Matthew 2:10–12; 14:33; 28:8–10, 16–17; John 9:35–38.
5. We will explore in detail the biblical witness of the divinity of the Holy Spirit in chapter 4.

while God was indeed one, there was also distinction within that oneness as represented in the three persons of God the Father, God the Son, and God the Holy Spirit.

The Church's Definitive Declaration of the Trinity

While the early church worshipped the Father, Son, and Holy Spirit, it wasn't until the First Council of Constantinople in the fourth century AD that the church developed accurate language for describing the Trinity. This was in response to the rise of heresy that denied the divinity of Christ and the Holy Spirit. To set into place the church's official and authoritative understanding of the revelation of God as three persons, theologians drew on three key concepts: (1) essence (*homoousion*), (2) personhood (*hypostasis*), and (3) mutual indwelling (*perichoresis*). These notions and the ideas they embodied enabled theologians to articulate an understanding of who God revealed himself to be in Scripture and Jesus while preserving the oneness yet three-part distinction of God. Let's explore each of these.

> Theologians drew on three key concepts to describe the Trinity: (1) essence (*homoousion*), (2) personhood (*hypostasis*), and (3) mutual indwelling (*perichoresis*).

Three Persons, One Essence (*homoousion*)

A fierce debate arose within the church in the early part of the fourth century over Jesus's divinity. While the church worshipped Jesus as God, there was concern among some that affirming Jesus as coequal, coeternal, and indivisibly united with God the Father would run the risk of diminishing the Father's divinity. To ensure that the Father maintained a special divine status that was superior to Jesus, some theologians suggested that Christ did not have the same divine nature as God the Father. Instead, it was proposed that he had a nature *similar* to (*homoiousian*) or *different* from (*heteroousion*) the divine nature of God the Father.

After much debate, the church affirmed that the biblical and apostolic witness was clear: Jesus has the *same* divine nature (*homoousion*) as God the Father. The problem with *heteroousion* ("different nature") is that it results in idolatry because the church would be worshipping a being less than divine, which the Scriptures prohibit. The problem with *homoiousian* ("similar nature") is that it results in polytheism. Christ having a similar nature as God the

Father means that there is more than one kind of deity, which would mean a plurality of deities. That would be polytheism, which the Bible also rules out.

homoiousian ("similar essence") = polytheism
heteroousion ("different essence") = idolatry

The church declared its affirmation of the apostolic and biblical witness of Christ as coequal, coeternal, indivisibly united, and having the same essence as God the Father in the Nicene Creed in AD 325.

> While the Council of Nicaea confirmed the divinity of Jesus, the church had to meet again at Constantinople to settle the divinity of the Holy Spirit.

Soon after the Council of Nicaea, similar questions arose regarding the divinity of the Holy Spirit, so the church met again, but this time in Constantinople (modern-day Istanbul) to settle the matter. Much like the debate over the divinity of Christ, the church affirmed that God revealed through Jesus in the Scriptures that the Holy Spirit is also coequal, coeternal, and indivisibly united with God the Father and God the Son, all of whom share the same divine essence.

Personhood (*hypostasis*)

A part of the discussion in working out that the Father, Son, and Holy Spirit were coeternal, coequal, indivisibly united, and sharing the same substance, was how to uphold the integrity of the oneness of God, yet with distinction. How could the church continue to affirm the apostolic witness that God was one yet clearly revealed himself as God the Father, God the Son, and God the Holy Spirit? As informed by Scripture and the Holy Spirit, leading theologians found the Greek concept of personhood (*hypostasis*) fitting for the task.

How we think of personhood today is different than how the ancients understood the notion of personhood. When we think of a person, we think of the individual first. What comes to mind is our unique personalities, giftings, genders, race, nationality, etc. In the ancient world and many cultures today, personhood was wrapped up in the *community*. Personhood was inseparable from the complex matrix of relationships with other persons. From this perspective, a person is not so much oriented around individuality, but rather it is relationships that define personhood.

The most obvious example of this principle is that persons would not exist without their biological parents. Their very being came out of a community of two others (i.e., mom and dad). In this sense, our existence as persons is others-referential. Further still, who are we other than our children's parents, friends, siblings, parents, coworkers, and so on? If you strip all these relationships away, there is no person left. This is why we can define "personhood" as *subsisting relationships*, meaning that *our relationships with other people determine our very being*. As persons, we don't *have* relationships; we *are* relationships.

This concept helps us think about how the Trinity can be three and one. God is three persons, one God. God the Father, God the Son, and God the Holy Spirit do not *have* relationships; they *are* relationships. The Father's personhood is wrapped up in his relationship with the Son and the Holy Spirit. There is no Father without the Son and the Holy Spirit. The same is true of the Son, whose personhood is constituted by his relationship with the Father and the Holy Spirit. There is no Son without the Father and the Holy Spirit. Finally, the Spirit's personhood is constituted by his relationship with the Son and the Father. There is no Spirit without the Father and the Son.

> The Spirit's personhood is constituted by his relationship with the Son and the Father.

This way of thinking about personhood as subsisting relationships has a "rotating" feel, leading us to the final concept of mutual indwelling (*perichoresis*).

Mutual Indwelling (*perichoresis*)

Jesus says in John 14:10: "Do you not believe that I am *in* the Father and the Father is *in* me? The words that I say to you I do not speak on my own authority, but the Father *who dwells in me* does his works" (italics added).[6] Here Jesus speaks of the mutually indwelling nature of his relationship with God the Father. Jesus is in God the Father, and God the Father is in Jesus.

The sonship of Jesus makes the same point. Jesus describes his relationship with the first person of the Trinity as a Father-Son relationship. The very nature of a Father-Son relationship is that there is not one without the other. As discussed in the previous section on personhood, a father is only a father if there is a child, and a child is only a child if there is a parent. There is a dynamic of reciprocal determination at work within the parent-child relationship. Another way of describing this dynamic is the language of *mutual indwelling.*

In John 20:22, Jesus breathes on his disciples and says, "Receive the Holy Spirit." As symbolized in the breath of Jesus, the Holy Spirit demonstrates that he dwells in Jesus. The Old Testament applies this same imagery to God the Father. Genesis 1:2 says that "the Spirit of God was hovering over the face of the waters." The psalmist says, "By the word of the Lord the heavens were made, and by the breath of his mouth all

> Mutual indwelling means that the loss of one always results in the collapse of the Trinity as a whole.

---

6. See also John 14:20.

their host" (33:6). The psalmist is saying that the Spirit of God that is hovering over the waters before God begins to create is the breath of God. This is affirmed in the Hebrew word for "spirit," which is the same word for "wind" or "breath." The Holy Spirit symbolized as the breath of God the Father and God the Son demonstrates that the Holy Spirit dwells within each of them, and each of them in the Holy Spirit.

Another way to look at mutual indwelling is unity without the loss of the individual. Mutual indwelling means that the loss of one always results in the collapse of the Trinity as a whole. Just like if there is no dad to join with mom, there is no child. If there is no Father, then there is no Son and Holy Spirit because there is an indivisibly united, rotating relationship between the three persons of the Trinity out of which the divine nature exists. Mutual indwelling is the means through which the ontological bond of fellowship is realized. Once again, the absence of one member of the Trinity not only results in the reduction from three to two, but the loss of divinity itself.

The Uniqueness of the Holy Spirit within the Trinity

Thus far, we have discussed the Trinity's shared nature, personhood as subsisting relations, and mutual indwelling. Against this backdrop, we can look at the uniqueness of the Holy Spirit and how he relates to the other two persons of the Trinity. We will first discuss the notion of the Holy Spirit as the third person of the Trinity and then the idea of eternal processions.

The Notion of Third

The Holy Spirit is coequal with God the Father and God the Son in both *essence* and *person-ness*. The Father is the source of the divine essence and a person, the eternally begotten Son is the image of the divine essence and a person, and the Holy Spirit proceeds from the Father's divine essence and is a person. The Holy Spirit is counted as *third*, then, not because he is of a lesser rank or different substance than the other two persons of the holy Trinity; nor is he third because he is not a person, for he is a person indeed. Nor do we use numbers in reference to the persons of the Trinity because they are fully adequate descriptors.[7]

> The Holy Spirit is coequal with God the Father and God the Son in both *essence* and *person-ness*.

---

7. For more on the problem of thirdness, see Kroll and Leidenhag, "On the Revelation of the Holy Spirit and the Problem of Thirdness" in *The Third Person of the Trinity: Explorations in Constructive Dogmatics*, eds. Oliver D. Crisp and Fred Sanders (Grand Rapids: Zondervan, 2020), 36–54.

Rather, the Holy Spirit is the third person of the Trinity because he proceeds from the Father *through the Son*. In other words, his sending and receiving *is mediated through the Son*. Thomas Torrance writes:

> Our receiving of the Spirit is objectively grounded in and derives from Christ who as the incarnate Son was anointed by the Spirit in his humanity and endowed with the Spirit without measure, not for his own sake (for he was eternally one in being with the Spirit in God) but for our sakes, and who then mediates the Spirit to us through himself.[8]

When the Father sends the Spirit into the world, it is through the Son and on the basis of the Son's redemptive work. The incarnation is for the sake of Pentecost and the latter is dependent upon the former. It is through union with Christ that the church receives the Spirit. The Holy Spirit is "third" because God the Father "gives" God the Son to the

> It is through union with Christ that the church receives the Spirit.

---

8. Thomas F. Torrance, *The Christian Doctrine of God: One Being Three Persons*, The Cornerstone Series (New York: T&T Clark, 1996), 148.

world, after which he sends the Holy Spirit through the Son and with the Son.⁹

Eternal Processions

The Nicene-Constantinopolitan Creed is very intentional in its language that the Holy Spirit *proceeds* from the Father and the Son. What does this mean? Gregg Allison answers that question concisely with this: "This [procession] does not mean that the Holy Spirit was created by them, or that his divine nature is derived from theirs, or that he is inferior, but it means that he is eternally dependent on them for his person-of-the-Spirit."¹⁰ We mentioned that the concept of personhood (*hypostasis*) means "subsisting relations," meaning that a person is only a person as they are in relationship

> In the simplest sense, "proceeds" simply means "sent." Beyond this, we must hit the mystery button.

---

9. This way of thinking about the Holy Spirit as the *third person* of the Trinity is focused on the Holy Spirit in his function pertaining to the Trinity's relationship with the creation (the economic Trinity, or God *ad extra*). There is debate within the church as the notion of thirdness regarding the Holy Spirit within the inner life of the holy Trinity (the immanent Trinity, or God *ad intra*). The details of that debate are far beyond the scope of this book.

10. Gregg R. Allison, "Eternal Processions" in *The Baker Compact Dictionary of Theological Terms* (Grand Rapids: Baker Books, 2016).

with other persons. The distinctness of the Holy Spirit within the Godhead is derived from his relationship with the Father and the Son. The distinctness of the Son from the Father and the Spirit is marked by the phrase "eternally begotten." Similarly, the distinctness of the Spirit is marked by the phrase "eternally proceeds." But what does it mean to proceed? In the simplest sense, "proceeds" simply means "sent." Beyond this, we must hit the mystery button. Gregory of Nazianzus writes:

> What then is Procession? Do you tell me what is the Unbegottenness of the Father, and I will explain to you the physiology of the Generation of the Son and the Procession of the Spirit, and we shall both of us be frenzy-stricken for prying into the mystery of God. And who are we to do these things, we who cannot even see what lies at our feet, or number the sand of the sea, or the drops of rain, or the days of Eternity, much less enter into the Depths of God, and supply an account of that Nature which is so unspeakable and transcending all words?[11]

Conclusion

The Old Testament witnesses to God's unicity. The New Testament affirms the witness of the oneness of God while

---

11. Gregory of Nazianzen, *Oration* 31, NPNF2 7:320.

further witnessing that Jesus and the Holy Spirit are also divine. In response to the rise of heretical teaching that Jesus and the Holy Spirit were either lesser deities (*homoiousion*) or not divine (*heteroousion*), the church definitively and unanimously affirmed the oneness of God with the distinction of three persons: the Father, the Son, and the Holy Spirit; the holy Trinity. The Trinitarian concept of "unity with distinction" is captured in the terms *homoousion* ("same substance"), *hypostasis* ("person"), and *perichoresis* ("mutual indwelling"). Within the Trinity, the Holy Spirit is the third person of the Trinity who eternally proceeds from the Father through the Son.

Why It Matters

Why does it matter that God is three persons and that the Holy Spirit eternally proceeds from the Father through the Son? It matters because we are made in the image of God. This means that the triune life of God is the model after which human life, fulfillment, purpose, and our very existence is based. If we don't understand that God is three persons, we will never understand what human life is all about. More specifically, because God is three persons, we can understand that

> Because God is three persons, we can understand that to be human is to be in self-giving love relationship with others. We are made not for ourselves but one another.

to be human is to be in self-giving love relationship with others. We are made not for ourselves but one another. Just as each member of the Trinity exists for the other, so it is with human life. As persons, we will find that the most important thing about us is our relationships with others. It is not our gender, race, nationality, or unique personalities. The most important thing about us, what makes you you, is relationships. We don't *have* relationships; we *are* relationships. Ultimately, it is our relationship with the Trinity that defines us.

Questions for Reflection and Discussion

1. What is the meaning of the phrase "subsisting relationships"?
2. How is the Holy Spirit distinct from the other persons of the holy Trinity?
3. What does the phrase "eternal processions" mean regarding the Holy Spirit?
4. Why do we refer to the Holy Spirit as the third person of the Trinity?

CHAPTER 4

The Holy Spirit Is God

God reveals in Scripture that the Holy Spirit is a divine person, meaning that he is coequal, coeternal, and indivisibly united with God the Father and God the Son; as the Nicene Creed states: "with the Father and the Son he is worshipped and glorified." But how do we conclude that the Holy Spirit is God? The Scriptures reveal that:

- The Holy Spirit has attributes that only God has;
- The Holy Spirit gives life;
- The Holy Spirit is called God;
- The Holy Spirit is referred to by divine titles; and
- The Holy Spirit manifests the divine Presence.

Let's explore each of these.

The Holy Spirit Has the Attributes of God

On the sixth day of the creation, God created humanity in his image. This means that humanity, to some extent, is like God. There are attributes of God that God *shares with humanity*. These are attributes like emotion, intelligence, will, etc. These shared attributes of God are known as the *communicable attributes* of God.

While God shares some of his attributes with humanity, humans are not like God in every way. There are specific attributes of God that are unique to him alone. These attributes include: eternality (God has no beginning or end), omnipresence (God is not limited by time or space), omniscience (God knows and understands all things and his judgments are perfect), and omnipotence (all-powerful). These are known as the *incommunicable attributes* of God. The Scriptures describe the Holy Spirit as having all the incommunicable attributes of God, which means that he must be divine.

The Holy Spirit Has No Beginning and No End (*Eternality*)

The first of the Holy Spirit's incommunicable divine attributes is his eternality. God alone is eternal. All created beings and things have a beginning. The creation didn't exist before God created it. While those in Christ have a life that will not end (John 3:16), all our lives have a beginning. This is not true of God. Even Jesus existed for an eternity before he became incarnate (John 1:1; 17:5; Rev. 22:13). John says in John 1:1: "In the beginning was the Word and the Word was with God and the Word was God." And as Jesus told those questioning him, "Before Abraham was, I am" (John 8:58).

Just as God has no beginning, he also has no end (Pss. 90; 43:10). Isaiah says: "Have you not known? Have you not heard? The LORD is the *everlasting God*" (40:28a, italics added). God has existed from eternity to eternity. God is not restricted by time because God alone is not a created being. He does not change (Ps. 102:27), does not age, and does not tire (Ps. 121:4).

> The Spirit is eternal: there was never a time that the Holy Spirit did not exist.

Hebrews 9:14 says that the Holy Spirit, as God, is eternal. It says: "how much more will the blood of Christ, who through the *eternal Spirit* offered himself without blemish to God, purify our conscience from dead works to serve the living God" (italics added). In other words, there was never a time that the Holy Spirit did not exist. We said in previous chapters that God tells Moses in Exodus 3:14 that he is the "I AM," which speaks to his eternality (among other things). This name is fitting for the Holy Spirit as well because he, as God, has no beginning and no end. He existed for eternity before the foundation of the world, and he will always be.

Together with God the Father and God the Son, the Holy Spirit is the alpha and the omega, the beginning and the end, the one who was, who is, and who is to come.

The Holy Spirit Is Everywhere (Omnipresence)

A second incommunicable divine attribute of the Holy Spirit is that he is everywhere (i.e., omnipresent). God alone is not bound by space because the divine presence is not limited or restricted in any way. If space is created, and the holy Trinity existed before creating space, God cannot be bound by space.

The apostle Paul says in Acts 17:28 that we "live and move and have our being" in God. This means that God contains all the creation in himself. There is nowhere that we can go where God is not. There is nowhere, even in the uttermost extremities of the universe, where God is absent. He pervades the creation. He is everywhere at once. God says in Jeremiah 23:23–24: "Am I a God at hand, declares the Lord, and not a God far away? Can a man hide himself in secret places so that I cannot see him? declares the Lord. Do I not fill heaven and earth? declares the Lord."

> There is nowhere, even in the uttermost extremities of the universe, where God is absent. He pervades the creation.

The Holy Spirit, as God, is everywhere, says the psalmist. Psalm 139:7–12 says:

> Where shall I go from your Spirit?
> > Or where shall I flee from your presence?
> If I ascend to heaven, you are there!
> > If I make my bed in Sheol, you are there!
> If I take the wings of the morning
> > and dwell in the uttermost parts of the sea,
> even there your hand shall lead me,
> > and your right hand shall hold me.
> If I say, "Surely the darkness shall cover me,
> > and the light about me be night,"
> even the darkness is not dark to you;
> > the night is bright as the day,
> > for darkness is as light with you.

By the inspiration of the Holy Spirit, the psalmist declares that there is nowhere he can go to escape the presence of the Holy Spirit. As God, the Holy Spirit is not absent from any part of the creation, which means that he is God.

The Holy Spirit Is All-Knowing (Omniscience)

God alone has unlimited knowledge. He knows everything. Jesus tells us that even the very hairs on our heads are numbered (Luke 12:7). God knows all the facts, figures, calculations, formulas, and solutions. The knowledge of God is so infinitely vast that the magnitude of the creation is nothingness in comparison. Isaiah says: "All the nations are as nothing before him, they are accounted by him as less than nothing and emptiness" (Isa. 40:17).

God doesn't just know everything, he also understands everything. His knowledge is comprehensive, integrated, and perfectly appropriated and ordered. Yes, he knows *what*, but he also knows *why* and *how*. Psalm 147:5 says: "Great is our Lord, and abundant in power; his understanding is beyond measure." His comprehension is inexhaustible. God is not simply an eternal database with all information; he perfectly understands the information and is the source of that information.

> God's knowledge is comprehensive, integrated, and perfectly appropriated and ordered.

God also has perfect wisdom. God alone is all-wise. His wisdom is inexhaustible. His decisions and judgments are perfectly sound and lack nothing. He does not make mistakes, overlooks no variables, and has no lapse in judgment. Proverbs 3:19–20 says: "The LORD by wisdom founded the earth; by understanding he established the heavens; by his knowledge the deeps broke open, and the clouds drop down the dew."

The Holy Spirit, says Paul, is omniscient. He says, "For the Spirit searches everything, *even the depths of God*. For who knows a person's thoughts except for the spirit of that person, who is in him? So also no one comprehends the thoughts of God except the Spirit of God" (1 Cor. 2:10–11, italics added). If the Holy Spirit can search the depths of God and comprehend the thoughts of God, then he, too, must be omniscient—an attribute of God alone. The Spirit's knowledge cannot be augmented because it lacks nothing. He knows the facts (Matt. 10:30) and has comprehensive understanding (Isa. 40:13–17) and perfect wisdom.

The Holy Spirit Is All-Powerful (Omnipotence)

Paul says that God's power is eternal (Rom. 1:20), meaning without limit. God can do all things that are consistent with his character. All his plans and purposes are perfectly fulfilled. Job says, "I know that you can do all things, and that *no purpose of yours can be thwarted*" (Job 42:2, italics added).

We also see the omnipotence of God in the titles for God in the Bible. The Old Testament calls God "God Almighty" (Gen. 17:1) and the "Lord of Hosts" (1 Sam. 1:3). "Lord of Hosts" refers to God's position of ultimate sovereignty over the supernatural beings of the unseen realm. In the New Testament, he is the "Almighty" (Rev. 1:8), meaning "all-powerful."

> Omnipotence means God can do all things that are consistent with his character.

In Genesis, God effortlessly creates without resistance or rebellion from external forces or persons. His decrees of "let there be" are utterly unchallenged. The psalmist speaks to the Holy Spirit's involvement in the omnipotent creative work of God in Psalm 104:30, saying: "When you send forth your Spirit, they are created, and you renew the face of the ground." The Hebrew verb here translated "created" is the same verb used in Genesis 1:1 where it says: "In the beginning, God created heavens and earth." The psalmist is saying, then, "When you send forth your Spirit, he is a part of that which only God can do."

It is by the power of the Holy Spirit that Jesus performs miracles, casts out demons, and has authority over Satan, who is the great dragon and "god of this world" (2 Cor. 4:4). Jesus says in Matthew 12:28–29: "But if it is by the Spirit of God that I cast out demons, then the kingdom of God has come upon you. Or how can someone enter a strong man's house and plunder his goods, unless he first binds the strong man? Then indeed he may plunder his house."

John reminds us that the Holy Spirit who indwells believers is greater than he who is in the world (1 John 4:4).

The Holy Spirit who constitutes and embodies the church is the operative force that advances the kingdom of God, against which the gates of hell cannot stand. The Holy Spirit indwells Christ, who is the light of the world that the darkness cannot overcome (John 1:4–5).

The Holy Spirit Gives Life

Directly related to the omnipotence of the Holy Spirit is that the Spirit creates life, which also attests to his divinity. In Romans 8:2, Paul calls the Holy Spirit the "Spirit of Life." In John 6:63, Jesus says: "It is the Spirit who gives life; the flesh is no help at all. The words that I have spoken to you are spirit and life."

> The power to create and sustain life are attributes of God alone.

The power to create and sustain life are attributes of God alone. Before God breathed the Holy Spirit into Adam, he was a lifeless form (Gen. 2:7). Similarly, the Holy Spirit brought Jesus's dead body back to life (Rom. 1:4), and it is the Holy Spirit who sustains the Christian's life in Christ (John 20:22). Jesus tells Nicodemus that unless one is "born of water and Spirit, he cannot enter the kingdom of God" (John 3:5). This means that the new birth that individuals experience in conversion is the work of the Holy Spirit. Jesus himself was conceived by the Holy Spirit (Matt. 1:18).

Romans 8 is a clear and powerful declaration of the life-giving ministry of the Holy Spirit. There we find the following statements from the apostle Paul:

- "For the law of the Spirit of life has set you free in Christ Jesus from the law of sin and death" (v. 2).
- "For to set the mind on the flesh is death, but to set the mind on the Spirit is life and peace" (v. 6).
- "But if Christ is in you, although the body is dead because of sin, the Spirit is life because of righteousness" (v. 10).
- "If the Spirit of him who raised Jesus from the dead dwells in you, he who raised Christ Jesus from the dead will also give life to your mortal bodies through his Spirit who dwells in you" (v. 11).
- "For if you live according to the flesh you will die, but if by the Spirit you put to death the deeds of the body, you will live" (v. 13).

The central idea in Romans 8 is that through Christ's redemptive work, the new age of the Spirit is now amongst us, and that age is marked by the new, sanctified life made possible through the Holy Spirit.

New Testament scholar N. T. Wright helpfully says this about these texts from Romans:

> the key contrast for the present passage [Rom. 8:1–11] is that between death and life: "life" is the golden

thread that runs through 8:1–11, the gift of God that the law wanted to give but could not, the gift that comes because God's Son has dealt with sin and death and God's life-giving Spirit has replaced sin as the indwelling power within God's people. The Promise of resurrection with which the passage concludes is not added for extra effect at the end of the paragraph. It is where the whole argument is leading.[1]

John Wesley beautifully describes the life-giving Presence of the Holy Spirit in believers, saying:

> the life of God in the soul of a believer is [. . .] *the continual inspiration of God's Holy Spirit*: God's breathing into the soul, and the soul's breathing back what it first receives from God; a continual action of God upon the soul, and re-action of the soul upon God; an unceasing presence of God, the loving, pardoning God, manifested to the heart, and perceived by faith; and an unceasing return of love, praise, and prayer, offering up all the thoughts of our hearts, all the words of our tongues, all the works of our hands, all our body, soul, and spirit,

---

[1] N. T. Wright, "Romans" in *The New Interpreter's Bible: A Commentary in Twelve Volumes*, Vol. 10 (Nashville: Abingdon, 2015), 574.

to be an holy sacrifice, acceptable unto God in Christ Jesus.[2]

The Holy Spirit is the Giver of Life, a title for God alone.

The Holy Spirit Is Called God

The Scriptures explicitly call the Holy Spirit "God." Acts 5 recounts the story of Ananias and Sapphira:

> But a man named Ananias, with his wife Sapphira, sold a piece of property, and with his wife's knowledge he kept back for himself some of the proceeds and brought only a part of it and laid it at the apostles' feet. But Peter said, "Ananias, why has Satan filled your heart to lie to *the Holy Spirit* and to keep back for yourself part of the proceeds of the land? While it remained unsold, did it not remain your own? And after it was sold, was it not at your disposal? Why is it that you have contrived this deed in your heart? You have not lied to man *but to God.*" (vv. 1–4, italics added)

---

2. John Wesley, "The Great Privilege of Those That Are Born of God" in *The Sermons of John Wesley: A Collection for the Christian Journey*, eds. Kenneth J. Collins and Jason E. Vickers (Nashville: Abingdon Press, 2013), 183.

In Peter's rebuke, he first says that Ananias lied to the Holy Spirit (v. 3), and then goes on to say that Ananias has "not lied to man, but to God" (v. 4), thereby calling the Holy Spirit "God." In sum, Peter says to Ananias, "You have lied to the Holy Spirit who is God." Fourth-century theologian Gregory of Nazianzus was defending the divinity of the Holy Spirit when he wrote: "Men . . . who so frighteningly placarded the guilty Ananias and Sapphira, when they lied to the Spirit, as 'liars to God not to man'—are those men, in your opinion, preaching that the Holy Spirit is God or that he is something else?"[3] Another great theologian and contemporary of Gregory, Basil the Great, also commented on this passage from Acts, saying: "This shows that to sin against the Holy Spirit is to sin against God. Understand from this that in every question, the Holy Spirit is indivisibly united with the Father and the Son."[4]

> "To sin against the Holy Spirit is to sin against God."

Jesus also teaches that one can commit blasphemy against the Holy Spirit and sin against the Holy Spirit, which is a category reserved for the divine (Matt. 12:31–32).[5]

---

3. Gregory of Nazianzus, *Orations* 31.30 (SVS 141).
4. Basil of Caesarea, "On the Holy Spirit" in *St. Basil: Letters and Select Works* (New York: Christian Literature Company, 1895) (*NPNF2*), 23.
5. See chapter 6 for a fuller explanation of blasphemy against the Holy Spirit.

Paul also calls the Holy Spirit "God" in 1 Corinthians 6:19–20 (cf. 1 Cor. 3:16). He writes: "Or do you not know that your body is a temple of the Holy Spirit within you, whom you have from God? You are not your own, for you were bought with a price. So glorify God in your body." Paul first says that the Holy Spirit dwells in the physical bodies of believers. He then goes on to command his readers to "glorify God in your body." Like the book of Acts, Paul makes the Holy Spirit parallel, or equivalent, with God.

The Holy Spirit Has Divine Titles

The biblical titles of the Holy Spirit also affirm his divinity. He is called:

- The Spirit of God (Gen. 1:2; Matt. 3:16)
- The Spirit of Yahweh (Isa. 11:2)
- The Spirit of the Lord (Luke 4:18; Acts 5:9)
- The Spirit of our God (1 Cor. 6:11)
- The Spirit of the Living God (2 Cor. 3:3)
- The Lord (2 Cor. 3:17–18)
- The Spirit of Christ (Rom. 8:9; 1 Peter 1:11)
- Spirit of Grace (Heb. 10:29)
- The Spirit of Truth (John 14:17; 15:26; 16:13; 1 John 4:6)
- The Spirit of Life (Rom. 8:2)

The Holy Spirit Manifests the Personal Presence of God

According to the Scriptures, the Holy Spirit manifests the personal Presence of God to the creation. As we noted in previous sections, God's presence is everywhere in the creation. At the same time, there are also special ways in which God makes his Presence known in the world. As A. W. Tozer puts it: "The presence and the manifestation of the presence are not the same. There can be the one without the other. God is here when we are wholly unaware of it. He is *manifest* only when and as we are aware of His presence."[6]

> David recognized the difference between the general presence of God and the personal Presence of God.

David recognized the difference between the general presence of God and the personal Presence of God. He says that the Holy Spirit is synonymous with the latter. David writes: "Cast me not away from your presence, *and take not your Holy Spirit from me*" (Ps. 51:11, italics added; also see Ps. 139:7–8). David does not deny that God's presence is everywhere in the creation. However, he is highlighting that God's Presence is available in special ways and that the Holy Spirit is the one who mediates that Presence. David

---

6. A. W. Tozer, *The Pursuit of God* (1948; repr. Abbotsford, WI: Aneko Press, 2015), 50.

says that if the Holy Spirit is not with him, then God is not with him. This is only possible if the Holy Spirit is divine.

We also see the Holy Spirit as the personal Presence of God in the tabernacle and the temple. In the Old Testament, the temple was the place of God's Presence and dwelling. In Exodus 19, God's Presence filled the tabernacle. His Presence was in the cloud by day and fire by night. It becomes apparent in the New Testament that the Presence of God as fire in the temple is the Holy Spirit.

We first see this in John's proclamation that Jesus will baptize with "the Spirit and with fire" (Matt. 3:11), which is fulfilled at Pentecost in Acts 2 when Christ pours out the Holy Spirit on the disciples in the Upper Room, and a tongue of fire rests over each of them. Acts 2:1–4 says:

> When the day of Pentecost arrived, they were all together in one place. And suddenly there came from heaven a sound like a mighty rushing wind, and it filled the entire house where they were sitting. And divided tongues as of fire appeared to them and rested on each one of them. And they were all filled with the Holy Spirit and began to speak in other tongues as the Spirit gave them utterance.

As we will discuss in a later chapter, this event is a reenactment of the moment in the desert when the glory of God descended on the tabernacle. The significance of this is that the Holy Spirit manifests the divine Presence of God, which is only possible if he is divine.

Conclusion

This chapter showed that the Bible teaches that the Holy Spirit is divine. We looked at the divine attributes of the Holy Spirit (i.e., all-powerful, all-knowing, not restricted by time and space), the divine titles of the Holy Spirit, and that for the Holy Spirit to truly represent the divine Presence, he must be God.

Why It Matters

> The entire point of Jesus's ministry was to restore the divine Presence in the heart of humanity *via* the Holy Spirit.

Why does it matter that the Holy Spirit is God? If the Holy Spirit is not God, then Jesus's birth, life, death, and resurrection save no one. The entire point of Jesus's ministry was to restore the divine Presence in the heart of humanity *via* the Holy Spirit. If the Holy Spirit is not God, it is something other than the divine Presence that indwells believers. If the Holy Spirit is not God, there is no divine, life-giving Presence in Christians. Only God can redeem the sinful heart of humans. Only the power and Presence of God can radically transform human nature by breaking the power of forgiven sin. The Holy

Spirit is the divine Person who accomplishes that through indwelling Christians. If he's not God, we are stuck living without the power to live free from sin, and sin and death, not Christ, still reign.

Questions for Reflection and Discussion

1. Name three divine attributes.
2. What does it mean that the Holy Spirit is eternal?
3. If the Holy Spirit is not God, then Jesus's redemptive work is not effective. Why?

CHAPTER 5

The Holy Spirit Is a Person

That the Holy Spirit manifests the personal Presence of God brings us to another essential aspect of the identity of the Holy Spirit: *the Holy Spirit is a person*, not an impersonal force. We can naturally sense the personhood of the Father and the Son in their titles. Sons and fathers are persons. But what about *pneuma* ("breath," "wind," "spirit")? Graham Cole points out that the imagery used to describe the Holy Spirit's activity among believers can lend it more to an impersonal force than a person. He writes:

> On the day of Pentecost, the Spirit's activity is "a sound like a mighty rushing wind" and "tongues as of fire" (Acts 2:2–3). The Spirit fills the disciples like a liquid (e.g., v. 4) and is poured out by the risen Christ like a liquid (v. 33). In the Paulines, the Spirit is likened to the firstfruits of a harvest (Rom. 8:23), a seal (Eph. 1:13), and a guarantee or down payment on a block of land (v. 14). So is

the Holy Spirit of God personal or an impersonal force from God?[1]

We will see that the Scriptures reveal that Holy Spirit: (1) has the attributes of a person and (2) manifests the Presence of God, who is a person, meaning that the Holy Spirit must be a person. This witness of the Scriptures is why the Nicene Creed definitively declares the personhood of the Holy Spirit in describing the Spirit as "the Giver of Life, who proceeds from the Father and the Son, who with the Father and the Son is adored and glorified, who has spoken through the prophets."

The Holy Spirit Has the Attributes of a Person

The Holy Spirit has attributes that only a person has in the Scriptures; namely, emotion and intelligence. Impersonal things such as a rock or wind have no such qualities. Rocks do not feel, think, or speak. The Holy Spirit, however, does because he is a person.

---

1. Graham A. Cole, *He Who Gives Life: The Doctrine of the Holy Spirit*, ed. John S. Feinberg, Foundations of Evangelical Theology (Wheaton, IL: Crossway Books, 2007), 65–66.

The Holy Spirit Has Emotions and Will

According to Isaiah 63:10 and Ephesians 4:30, we can grieve the Holy Spirit. Isaiah 63:10 says: "But they rebelled and grieved his Holy Spirit; therefore he turned to be their enemy, and himself fought against them." The prophet here describes how Israel responded to God's goodness and faithfulness in rescuing them from Egyptian slavery. Israel was a nation of abused and oppressed slaves who cried out to God for help. God, in his compassion, heard their crying and groaning and brought them out of Egypt. Isaiah writes: "In all their affliction he was afflicted, and the angel of his presence saved them; in his love and in his pity he redeemed them; he lifted them up and carried them all the days of old" (Isa. 63:9). God suffered because his people suffered. His compassion drove him to rescue them from their plight. As a reward for his kindness, they rejected him. This rejection grieved him. More specifically, this rejection grieved his Holy Spirit.

> An impersonal force doesn't have compassion. A wind does not have pity.... But Israel hurt and grieved the Holy Spirit.

This whole account is deeply personal. The Israelites did more than resist God. They rebelled against him and rejected his compassion, his mercy, and even his redeeming Presence among them. An impersonal force doesn't have compassion. A wind does not have pity. You can't grieve a chair, a car, a watch, or a cup. But Israel hurt and grieved the Holy Spirit. This whole scenario is only possible if the Holy Spirit is a person who has a will, intelligence, and emotion.

The author of Hebrews says: "How much worse punishment, do you think, will be deserved by the one who has trampled underfoot the Son of God, and has profaned the blood of the covenant by which he was sanctified, and has *outraged the Spirit* of grace?" (Heb. 10:29, italics added). The word the English Standard Version translates here as "outrage," other versions translate as "insult." Outrage and insult result from disapproval, which is only possible with desire and intelligence. Insult involves disrespect and scorn. Can you insult and scorn an impersonal force? In its context, Thomas Schreiner writes: "Those who reject the blood of Jesus do not merely sin against the Spirit. They insult and despise the Spirit."[2]

> "Those who reject the blood of Jesus do not merely sin against the Spirit. They insult and despise the Spirit."

Furthermore, the Holy Spirit can be pleased and satisfied. Acts 15:28–29 says:

> "For it has seemed good to the Holy Spirit and to us to lay on you no greater burden than these

---

2. Thomas R. Schreiner, *Hebrews*, eds. T. Desmond Alexander, Thomas R. Schreiner, and Andreas J. Köstenberger, Evangelical Biblical Theology (Bellingham, WA: Lexham Press, 2021), 326.

requirements: that you abstain from what has been sacrificed to idols, and from blood, and from what has been strangled, and from sexual immorality. If you keep yourselves from these, you will do well. Farewell."

In other words, the Holy Spirit wanted something specific; namely, that those in question abstain from particular activities. Do impersonal forces make moral assessments? Do they have a will? Impersonal forces are acted upon; they do not act out of a will or desire. The Holy Spirit can be grieved, insulted, and has a will, demonstrating that he is a person. Any suggestion that these verses speak figuratively about the Holy Spirit ignores the text's plain meaning and the church's history of Spirit-led interpretation through the centuries.

The Holy Spirit Has Intelligence

The Holy Spirit's intelligence also demonstrates his personhood. The Holy Spirit's intelligence is evidenced in several ways. One way is covered in the previous section on the omniscience of the Holy Spirit. An impersonal force does not have understanding, knowledge, and wisdom. Mere wind cannot "[search] everything, even the depths of God" (1 Cor. 2:10).

The Holy Spirit *speaks,* which also demonstrates his consciousness and intelligence.

- "And when they bring you to trial and deliver you over, do not be anxious beforehand what you are to say, but say whatever is given you in that hour, *for it is not you who speak, but the Holy Spirit.*" (Mark 13:11, italics added).
- "While they were worshipping the Lord and fasting, *the Holy Spirit said*, 'Set apart for me Barnabas and Saul for the work to which I have called them'"[3] (Acts 13:2–3, italics added).
- "And *the Spirit said* to Philip, 'Go over and join this chariot'" (Acts 8:29, italics added).
- "And coming to us, he took Paul's belt and bound his own feet and hands and said, '*Thus says the Holy Spirit*, "This is how the Jews at Jerusalem will bind the man who owns this belt and deliver him into the hands of the Gentiles"'" (Acts 21:11, italics added).
- "*Now the Spirit expressly says* that in later times some will depart from the faith by devoting themselves to deceitful spirits and teachings of demons" (1 Tim. 4:1, italics added).
- "He who has an ear, let him hear what *the Spirit says* to the churches. To the one who conquers I will grant to eat of the tree of life, which is in the paradise of God" (Rev. 2:7, italics added).

---

3. Cf. 2 Peter 1:21.

An impersonal force does not speak. It can move and be moved, but it cannot speak intelligently or coherently. Speech expresses thoughts and feelings, which impersonal forces do not have.

The Holy Spirit Manifests the Personal Presence of God

Jesus tells his disciples not to be troubled because even though he must leave them, he would send them a Helper in his place (John 16:7). For the Holy Spirit to fulfill this promise, he must be another of the same kind as Jesus, who is a person. If the Holy Spirit is not a person, he cannot be an adequate substitute for Jesus. Roger Olson writes:

> The Christian gospel is that God came among people in Jesus Christ—"Immanuel"—"God with us." It also includes the unity of God: "Hear O Israel, the Lord our God is one Lord." It also includes the presence of God within his people: the Spirit indwelling and empowering Christians.[4]

If the Holy Spirit is not a person, he cannot be an adequate substitute for Jesus after his ascension.

---

4. Roger E. Olson and Christopher A. Hall, *The Trinity*, Guides to Theology (Grand Rapids: W. B. Eerdmans, 2002), 3.

To be the Spirit of Christ that makes Christ's Presence forever with the church, the Holy Spirit must be a person.

Conclusion

This chapter established that the Bible reveals that the Holy Spirit is a person, not an impersonal force. We saw that the Holy Spirit has the attributes of a person (i.e., emotions, will, and intelligence) and that for the Holy Spirit to be a substitute for Jesus, he must be a person.

Why It Matters

It matters that the Holy Spirit is a person for the same reason that it matters that the Holy Spirit is God. If the Holy Spirit is not a divine person, then what Jesus sought to accomplish on the cross failed. The whole point of Jesus's life, death, and resurrection was to restore what was lost in the garden of Eden: the personal Presence of God in the life of people. God created humans to be in intimate fellowship with him. God's desire was to be bonded in love with his people, just as he's bonded together in love within himself (i.e., Father, Son, and Holy Spirit). The Scriptures compare this bond of love to marriage. God wanted to be a husband to humanity. This means sharing in personal Presence. When we exist in a proper, personal relationship with God, we are fully human, which is why when the divine Presence is lost, everything falls apart. The human heart becomes bent, twisted, perverse, unnatural, and far from God's intent. Jesus came to reconcile the relationship between God and people. Based on Jesus's reconciling work, the Holy Spirit is gifted to us. And, if the Holy Spirit is not a person, he cannot mediate the personal Presence of God to us, and we remain in the same condition that we were in before.

> God's desire was to be bonded in love with his people, just as he's bonded together in love within himself.

Jesus promised to be with his followers always (Matt. 28:20). He told them not to be dismayed that he would leave them because he would send another in his place (John 16:7). If the Holy Spirit is not a person, this was all a lie. For the Holy Spirit to indeed be the Presence of Jesus with believers, he must be a person. To truly be with his followers always through the Holy Spirit, the Holy Spirit must be of the same kind that Jesus is: a divine person.

Questions for Reflection and Discussion

1. What is the difference between a person and an impersonal force?
2. If the Holy Spirit is just an impersonal force, then the redeeming work of Jesus was not effective. Why?

3. What are two personal attributes of the Holy Spirit that are revealed in the Scriptures?
4. The Scriptures say on many occasions that the Holy Spirit speaks. What does this have to do with his personhood?

PART II

The Ministry of the Holy Spirit

The ministry of the Holy Spirit is to unify believers with Christ by restoring the person Presence of God to humanity on the merits of Christ's redeeming work. More specifically, Christ's work aims to put right (i.e., redeem) God's original plan to coinhabit the creation with the human heart as his dwelling place. By applying the work of Christ, the Holy Spirit, with the self-affirming, grace-enabled participation of the believer, restores the fellowship between humanity and the triune God. Because being is constituted through fellowship and mutual indwelling, the restoration of this relationship results in a spiritual birth and the regeneration of the image of God in people. This section will develop these concepts by exploring:

1. The ministry of the Holy Spirit within the way of salvation.
2. The ministry of the Holy Spirit in the church.
3. The Holy Spirit and end times.
4. The Holy Spirit and the Holy Life.

PART II

The Ministry of the Holy Spirit

CHAPTER 6

The Holy Spirit and Salvation

In considering the role of the Holy Spirit in salvation, we must first have a clear understanding of what salvation is. While salvation is simple and straightforward in some ways (i.e., reconciliation with God), it is rather complex in other ways. Yes, salvation involves a change in status (guilty to innocent), but it is also radical inner transformation (restoration of the image of God). Yes, there are key moments in salvation (conviction, repentance, justification, regeneration, and glorification), but it is also a journey (sanctification). Yes, salvation is a thing, but it's also a relationship.

On a more practical level, and using a biblical example, we can see the complexity of salvation when comparing Peter's and Paul's conversion stories. Paul's conversion was very dramatic and concentrated in the specific moment on the road to Damascus (Acts 9). But when was Peter saved? Was it when he obeyed Jesus by leaving behind his nets to follow him (Matt. 4:18–22)? Was it when he exercised faith and confessed that Jesus was the Christ, the Son of the living God (Matt. 16:13–20)? Was it when he told Jesus he loved him after the resurrection (John 21:15–19)? Or was it when he experienced the new birth and was filled with the Holy Spirit at Pentecost (Acts 2)? The point—once again—is that salvation is complex.

> The Holy Spirit is at work in restoring the image of God in us as we walk with him in a redeemed relationship.

One helpful way that Christian theologians have simplified thinking and talking about salvation is *as a process with ordered steps* known as the *order of salvation*. While there are various versions of the order of salvation within different Christian traditions, the one we will use here is as follows: (1) grace, (2) conviction, (3) repentance, (4) justification, (5) regeneration, (6) sanctification, and (7) glorification.

This order of salvation provides a concise and manageable way into understanding the role of the Holy Spirit in salvation. We will see in this chapter that the Holy Spirit applies the work of Jesus in the lives of individual believers and is active in the entire process of salvation, from administering the grace that softens the iron-clad human heart to bodily resurrection. In sum, we will see that the Holy Spirit is at work in restoring the image of God in us as we walk with him in a redeemed relationship.

Prevenient Grace: The Spirit of Grace

The first step in salvation is grace. Yes, the grace of God is the basis of salvation as a whole, but there is a particular kind of grace that prepares hearts that the disease of sin has hardened to receive the good gift of salvation. This preparing grace that draws us to Jesus is called "prevenient grace." John Wesley described prevenient grace as "the first wish to please God, the first dawn of light concerning His will, and the first slight transient conviction of having sinned against him."[1]

The Bible repeatedly describes the Israelites—who are a representative of *all humanity*—as stubborn and rebellious:

- "And the LORD said to Moses, 'I have seen this people, and behold, it is a stiff-necked people'" (Ex. 32:9).
- "Know, therefore, that the LORD your God is not giving you this good land to possess because of your righteousness, for you are a stubborn people" (Deut. 9:6).
- "Furthermore, the LORD said to me, 'I have seen this people and behold, it is a stubborn people'" (Deut. 9:13).

---

1. John Wesley, "On Working Out Our Own Salvation" in *The Sermons of John Wesley: A Collection for the Christian Journey*, eds. Kenneth J. Collins and Jason E. Vickers (Nashville: Abingdon Press, 2013), 66.

- "You have been rebellious against the Lord from the day that I knew you" (Deut. 9:24).
- "Circumcise therefore the foreskin of your heart, and be no longer stubborn" (Deut. 10:16).
- "For I know how rebellious and stubborn you are. Behold, even today while I am yet alive with you, you have been rebellious against the Lord. How much more after my death!" (Deut. 31:27).
- "And that they should not be like their fathers, a stubborn and rebellious generation,
  a generation whose heart was not steadfast, whose spirit was not faithful to God" (Ps. 78:8).
- "Because I know that you are obstinate, and your neck is an iron sinew, and your forehead brass" (Isa. 48:4).
- "But the house of Israel will not be willing to listen to you, for they are not willing to listen to me: because all the house of Israel have a hard forehead and a stubborn heart" (Ezek. 3:7).

This hard-hearted condition makes it so that even if God were to offer us the gift of reconciliation, we would foolishly reject it. We need grace to soften our hearts so that we can arrive at a place of self-awareness. Reconciliation requires acknowledgment of betrayal, and grace leads us to the place of acknowledgment.

So where does the Holy Spirit come in when it comes to prevenient grace that softens our hearts? The hard-hearted condition results from buying wholesale into the lie that God is not trustworthy. Being closed off to the truth that God is good and faithful is the work of the Deceiver (2 Cor. 4:4). The hardness of the heart is the result of firm belief in the lies of the Accuser. The Holy Spirit, the Spirit of Truth (John 16:13), exposes this lie and weakens its power. Going back to the garden of Eden, the serpent, the one who was lying from the beginning, accused God of being the liar. The serpent's deception cast a shadow on the character of God to corrupt his relationship with the original humans. The serpent's goal was to lead humanity to betray God. While death came through deception, truth brings light, life, and redemption (John 8:32; 14:6). By pointing to the cross, the Holy Spirit diffuses that heart-hardening lie and assures us of the perfect love and faithfulness of God. The Holy Spirit points to the life, death, and resurrection of Jesus to dispel the lie that keeps human hearts cold. The grace of the Spirit awakens conviction. Timothy Tennent writes:

> As Christians, we understand that we have the capacity to recognize moral categories because we are endowed with the image of God and the empowering presence of the Holy Spirit. We also recognize that the Spirit is a universal channel of grace to the whole of creation, bearing witness to the creation (Rom. 1:19), speaking in human consciences (Rom. 2:15), and restraining the full manifestation of evil (2 Thess. 2:7). Jesus himself bears witness to the

universal work of the Spirit, who convicts the world of sin and draws people to Christ (John 6:44; 16:8).[2]

The Holy Spirit softens the human heart by revealing the truth about God, particularly his love and trustworthiness, in pointing the world to Jesus and the cross. Grace enables the Spirit's heart-softening work. The Holy Spirit, through grace, not only transforms hearts in the moment of receiving the gift of saving faith but also prepares the believer to receive the gift. Hard and rebellious hearts must become soft, sympathetic, responsive, generous, and charitable to receive the gift of faith. Without grace, sinners are unable to choose the excellent gift of salvation. Thomas McCall says: "While sinful humans remain free, apart from the grace of the Holy Spirit they are unable to choose good. By the grace of the Holy Spirit, however, they are truly enabled to choose righteousness and goodness in faith and obedience."[3] In sum, even though we have rejected and betrayed him, God the Father sends God the Son after us in relentless pursuit, and that steadfast love of God melts

> Without Holy Spirit–enabled grace, sinners are unable to choose the excellent gift of salvation.

---

2. Timothy C. Tennent, *For the Body: Recovering a Theology of Gender, Sexuality, and the Human Body* (Grand Rapids: Zondervan, 2020), 13.
3. Thomas H. McCall, *Against God and Nature: The Doctrine of Sin* (Wheaton, IL: Crossway, 2019), 298.

our icy hearts. It is the self-sacrificing love of God that comes to find us in the wilderness of our rebellion.

Blasphemy Against the Holy Spirit: Resisting the Spirit of Truth

We can best understand blasphemy against the Holy Spirit within this context of grace as the first step in salvation. Jesus says, "Therefore I tell you, every sin and blasphemy will be forgiven people, but the blasphemy against the Spirit will not be forgiven. And whoever speaks a word against the Son of Man will be forgiven, but whoever speaks against the Holy Spirit will not be forgiven, either in this age or the age to come" (Matt. 12:31–32). On the surface, this statement seems contradictory to other New Testament teachings that all sin is forgivable for those who repent (1 John 1:9), and even the testimony of the apostle Paul (1 Tim. 2:13).

So what is blasphemy against the Holy Spirit? Blasphemy against the Holy Spirit is a heart-posture of absolute resistance to the Holy Spirit's heart-softening work. Simply put, those who resist the Holy Spirit cannot be saved. Resisting the Spirit means fighting the move toward conviction, repentance, forgiveness, regeneration, inner transformation, and resurrection. Those who oppose

> Blasphemy against the Holy Spirit is a heart-posture of absolute resistance to the Holy Spirit's heart-softening work.

the Holy Spirit cannot possibly believe in their hearts and confess that Jesus is Lord. Such a confession is only possible through the empowerment of the Holy Spirit. Paul says in 1 Corinthians 12:3: "Therefore I want you to understand that no one speaking in the Spirit of God ever says, 'Jesus is accursed!' and no one can say 'Jesus is Lord' except in the Holy Spirit."

Can God turn Saul into Paul? Yes! Can God dramatically break into the life of a hard-hearted, stiff-necked rebel and shock them into a full embrace of his goodness and love? Absolutely. Even in these scenarios, however, love is never coerced. Love must be mutual. Love requires willful cooperation and reciprocity. The Holy Spirit enables us to love God back. Resisting the Holy Spirit makes loving God impossible.

Conviction: The Spirit of Truth

In the first step of salvation (prevenient grace), the Holy Spirit—the Spirit of Truth—exposes the lie that God is not trustworthy. In the second step of salvation (conviction), the Holy Spirit exposes the lie that humans are not sinners. Jesus promised that the Holy Spirit would convict the world of sin (John 16:8). But what is conviction? Conviction is regret and remorse for sin that comes with the grace-enabled awareness that one is a sinner. Twentieth-century theologian Karl Barth writes:

> Man is corrupt even in his self-understanding, even in the knowledge of his corruption. He cannot see, therefore, beyond the inner conflict and its purely relative compass. He can never really see his sin, and himself as the man of sin. He cannot turn to a true knowledge of his corruption, but only evade it. God and His revelation and faith are all needed if He is to realise the accusation and judgment and condemnation under which he stands, and the transgression and ensuing need in which he exists.[4]

Sin is so deeply embedded in us and our environment that we cannot possibly conceive of the fact that we are culpable without the help of the Holy Spirit. It is simply impossible to admit that we have a sin problem. Our natural posture is to see ourselves as victims rather than treacherous rebels. Adam's response to God's accusation was, "She made me do it." We naturally blame all our problems on other people. Sin makes it impossible for us to come to grips with the sins we have committed and, even more so, our sin-diseased nature. Our inward bent makes it impossible to see ourselves (and

> The Holy Spirit helps us see ourselves as God sees us.

---

4. Karl Barth, *Church Dogmatics* IV/2: *The Doctrine of Reconciliation* (London: T&T Clark, 1958), 379.

others) straight. Our hearts are not only stubborn but also crooked and perverse. Because of sin, we are depraved to the point of delusion when it comes to who we believe ourselves to be.

Penetrating the iron-clad, prideful human heart is something only God can do. Based on prevenient grace, this is what the Holy Spirit does. The Holy Spirit helps us see ourselves as God sees us. The Holy Spirit brings light to our darkness and truth to our sin-saturated delusion. The Holy Spirit opens our ears to hear and eyes to see who we truly are: stiff-necked defiant rebels against God.

The deception that you're not a sinner only comes to light once the Holy Spirit shows us the character of God; namely, his trustworthiness and love, by pointing to the cross. By suffering and dying for his enemies, Jesus puts on display the steadfast, truly selfless love of God. Such love on display reveals our selfishness. McCall writes:

> We can begin to understand sin rightly only in relation to God—and thus to know sin better is to know God better, to better understand sin is to better understand the justice, righteousness, and holiness of God. And to better understand sin is to better understand the glorious mercy of the triune God whose nature is holy love.[5]

---

5. McCall, *Against God and Nature*, 31.

As the Holy Spirit reveals the goodness of God by pointing to Jesus and the cross, humanity's rebellion is exposed as sin. When rebels witness the goodness and holiness of God, there can be a sense of regret and remorse for sin.

The sin-illuminating ministry of the Holy Spirit is evident in the symbol of fire (Acts 2:1-4). The Holy Spirit, like fire, reveals. One of the fatal mechanisms of sin is that it remains hidden. It thrives in the dark. By hiding, sin convinces sinners that there is nothing wrong. The voice whispers, "Sin is the norm." Sin makes sure that we stay in the habit of measuring behavior, attitudes, emotions, and thoughts against other sinners rather than against Jesus. First John 1:8 says: "If we say that we have no sin, we deceive ourselves, and the truth is not in us." The illumination of the Holy Spirit in our lives opens our eyes to see that we are sinners. Once the goodness of God comes into our midst, so does the awareness of our sinfulness (Isa. 6). The apostle Paul writes to the Ephesians:

> One of the fatal mechanisms of sin is that it remains hidden. It thrives in the dark.

> Now this I affirm and insist on in the Lord: you must no longer live as the Gentiles live, in the futility of their minds. *They are darkened in their understanding*, alienated from the life of God because of their ignorance and hardness of heart. They have lost all sensitivity and have abandoned themselves

> to licentiousness, greedy to practice every kind of impurity. That is not the way you learned Christ! For surely you have heard about him and were taught in him, as truth is in Jesus. You were taught to put away your former way of life, your old self, corrupt and deluded by its lusts, and to be renewed *in the spirit of your minds*, and to clothe yourselves with the new self, created according to the likeness of God in true righteousness and holiness. (4:17–24 NRSVCE, italics added)

Paul points out that sinful behavior originates in the mind and heart. Paul describes the contrast between the empty minds of pagans and Christians who have "learned," "heard," and were "taught." As the illuminating fire, the Holy Spirit brings light to darkened minds and hearts; he reveals God's will to believers (John 14:26). The Holy Spirit is how believers can know what God wants and expects. Paul says in Romans 12:2: "Do not be conformed to this world, but be transformed by the renewal of your mind, that by testing you may discern what is the will of God, what is good and acceptable and perfect."

Paul also points out in the previous passage from Ephesians that having a darkened mind is synonymous with alienation from God (v. 18). First John 1:5–7 says:

> This is the message we have heard from him and proclaim to you, that God is light and in him there

is no darkness at all. If we say that we have fellowship with him while we are walking in darkness, we lie and do not do what is true; but if we walk in the light as he himself is in the light, we have fellowship with one another, and the blood of Jesus his Son cleanses us from all sin. (NRSVCE)

In other words, being forgiven of sin without being filled with the Holy Spirit is *less than* God's intentions for humanity. The human problem begins with the human heart's separation from God. As the Holy Spirit restores the Presence of God internally to humans, the sun rises on the human heart.

> The Holy Spirit imparts the righteousness of Christ to the believer.

The Holy Spirit not only reveals *sins*, but he also reveals that *sin is imbedded in our nature*. Paul highlights in Romans 7 that the Old Testament law draws out hidden sin; sin "came alive" because of the commands of God (v. 9). The Holy Spirit not only uncovers the human inability to overcome sin, but also reveals that the human condition is the distortion of human nature itself. The absence of God from the human heart corrupts the human condition to the point that when something as good and pure as the law of God comes along, rather than correcting the problem, humanity looks to it as a source for ideas on what not to do. In short, the Old Testament law arouses the carnal nature (v. 5).

We learn from the unusual reality of desires aroused by the law that we are incorrigibly rebellious. Sin is not so much about fulfilling the desires of the flesh as it is about rebellion. Rebellion is the most gratifying desire of the flesh to satisfy. We love showing the world that we are our own master and free, independent beings. It is the fallen human nature to push back, to resist. How would sinners discover this if there were no law to attempt to reign over them? It is by the establishment of rules over sinners that the natural impulse to rebel is aroused.

The Holy Spirit's work in revealing our diseased nature leads to an awareness of the need for a healed and renewed nature in Christ. The Holy Spirit not only brings an awareness of the need for forgiveness but ultimately a rebirth, both of which the Holy Spirit accomplishes in the believer's life. By dwelling in believers and convicting hearts of sin, and empowering obedience, the Holy Spirit imparts the righteousness of Christ to the believer. The Holy Spirit delivers from the condemnation of being held captive to an inner twistedness as Paul describes in Romans 6:1–11. In this passage, Paul is not merely addressing escape from the final judgment; he also addresses the reality of present deliverance from the destructive behavior generated out of a depraved heart. Paul is talking about the indwelling of the Holy Spirit that is able not only to forgive sins but to restore the image of God in humanity. The image of God restored in humanity (i.e., holiness) is a witness to the moral character of God in the world.

Repentance: The Holy Spirit Brings Humility

Repentance is a 180-degree turn away from sin and toward the Presence of God. Repentance is ceasing to resist the truth. Repentance, by definition, is a zealous, relentless change that is required for salvation, and it underscores that salvation is ultimately about being restored to fellowship with God. The Holy Spirit not only administers grace to convict hearts, but he also empowers the believer's cooperation to abandon the way of sin to live a life of abandon to God through repentance.

> Repentance, by definition, is a zealous, relentless change that is required for salvation, and it underscores that salvation is ultimately about being restored to fellowship with God.

Repentance Is a Zealous, Resolute Change

Repentance is distinct from conviction. Conviction is regret and remorse that confronts the conscience by the grace-enabled awareness of sin. One can be convicted yet not turn from their ways. One can regret their sin but fail to cease striving against the truth. Repentance is a turning from sin. Repentance ceases from sin and begins with the inner resolve to yield to God. Repentance is not merely a turning from sinful behavior. It starts with the resolution of the heart; it begins with submission. That submission leads to the abandonment of the spirit of rebellion against God. The fruit of repentance is ceasing to sin and committing to love (Matt. 3:8).

Such a thing must be purposeful, determined, and unwavering. Repentance in the Old Testament means turning one's face away in the opposite direction (Ezek. 14:6). The persistent nature of repentance is pervasive in the Scriptures:

- "If they repent with *all their heart* and with *all their soul* in the land of their enemies" (1 Kings 8:48, italics added).
- "When he killed them, they sought him; they repented and sought God *earnestly*" (Ps. 78:34, italics added).
- "Therefore say to the house of Israel, Thus says the Lord God: Repent and turn away from your idols, and turn away your faces from *all* your abominations" (Ezek. 14: 6, italics added).
- "Therefore I will judge you, O house of Israel, every one according to his ways, declares the Lord God. Repent and turn from *all* your transgressions, lest iniquity be your ruin" (Ezek. 18:30, italics added).

As Jesus puts it: "No one can serve two masters, for either he will hate the one and love the other, or he will be devoted to the one and despise the other. You cannot serve God and money" (Matt. 6:24). Repentance is abandoning one master for another. Anything less than complete abandonment of sin is not repentance.

Repentance Is Required for Salvation

As David puts it: "If a man does not repent, God will whet his sword; he has bent and readied his bow" (Ps. 7:12). If rebellion against God is the root of sin and at the heart of the sinful condition, then repentance is necessary for redemption. Restoration and reconciliation must be self-affirmed through an intentional turning back, which is why Jesus says, "I tell you; but unless you repent, you will all likewise perish" (Luke 13:3). Isaiah says: "Zion shall be redeemed by justice, and those in her who repent, by righteousness" (Isa. 1:27). Even the chosen people of God must repent to be redeemed.

The Ministry of John the Baptist

John the Baptist's ministry of repentance affirms that repentance is required for salvation. John prepares the way of the Lord through a call to repentance. Jesus's ministry begins with a call to repentance (Mark 1:15). Mark's gospel begins this way: "The beginning of the gospel of Jesus Christ, the Son of God. As it is written in Isaiah the prophet, 'Behold, I send my messenger before your face, who will prepare your way'" (Mark 1:1–2). If the beginning of the good news of Jesus is repentance, then without it, there is no good news.

John notes the distinction between those who receive Jesus and those who reject Jesus. John 1:11–13 says: "He came to his own, and his own people did not receive him. But *to all who did receive him, who believed in his name, he gave the right to become children of God*, who were born, not of blood nor of the will of the flesh nor of the will of man, but of God" (italics added).

> Receiving Jesus means turning away from sin and turning to him.

Receiving Jesus means turning away from sin and turning to him. Those who receive Jesus repent from their rebellion against him as the one through whom the world was made. Not receiving Jesus as the way, the truth, and the life is a failure to cease striving against the truth. Repentance is the embrace of truth in Jesus Christ. This means that those who refuse to repent are condemned.

That salvation requires grace-enabled, Spirit-empowered repentance means that God is just in condemning the unrepentant. While Christ was put forth as a propitiation for sin (Rom. 3:25; Heb. 2:17; 1 John 4:10), the gift of salvation still must be actively received. In Jesus's own words: "I have not come to call the righteous but sinners to repentance" (Luke 5:32).[6]

The Holy Spirit Enables Repentance

Jesus says, "No one can come to me unless the Father who sent me draws him. And I will raise him up on the last day" (John 6:44). He also says, "This is why I told you that no one can come to me unless it is granted him by the Father" (John 6:65). Turning back to God is not a human work that earns salvation. Repentance is the work of the Holy Spirit by grace through faith. Grace enables the believer to cooperate with the Holy Spirit's empowering of repentance. Individuals on their own and in their fallenness are unable to repent. John Barclay points out that "Paul has diagnosed the human heart as senseless . . . hardened, and completely incapable of repentance."[7] In commenting on blasphemy against the Holy Spirit, Thomas Oden writes: "This sin instantly places the self beyond the range of forgiveness,

> Turning back to God is not a human work that earns salvation. Repentance is the work of the Holy Spirit by grace through faith.

---

6. Cf. Luke 15:7

7. John M. G. Barclay, *Paul and the Gift* (Grand Rapids, MI; Cambridge, U.K.: William B. Eerdmans Publishing Company, 2015), 463-64.

because every step toward repentance and faith is enabled by the Holy Spirit."[8]

Repentance is dying to self, which is opposed to humanity's inward, self-centered bent. Jesus says, "For whoever would save his life will lose it, but whoever loses his life for my sake will find it" (Matt. 16:25). Paul's command for the Philippians to imitate Christ in his selflessness, as demonstrated in his perfect obedience (Phil. 2), is impossible to obey without the supernatural empowerment of the Holy Spirit.

Acts 11:18 says: "When they heard these things they fell silent. And they glorified God, saying, 'Then to the Gentiles also God has granted repentance that leads to life.'"[9] God *gives repentance* to sinners. Sinners do not (because they cannot) muster up the strength on their own to repent. Sinners repent only by the supernatural enabling of the Holy Spirit. Repentance, like faith, is a *gift*.

All Are Called to Repent

As the bearers of the image of God, all people are called to repent. God wills that all be saved. "God so loved the world"—not some—"that he gave his only Son" (John 3:16). Jesus said, "Thus it is written, that the Christ should suffer

---

8. Thomas C. Oden, *Life in the Spirit: Systematic Theology, Vol. III* (San Francisco: HarperSanFrancisco, 1992), 22.

9. See also 2 Timothy 2:25.

and on the third day rise from the dead, and that repentance for the forgiveness of sins should be proclaimed in his name to all nations, beginning from Jerusalem" (Luke 24:46–47, italics added). Like Christ's atoning work, the call to repentance is not limited to the elect, for "He is the propitiation for our sins, and not for ours only but also for the sins of the whole world" (1 John 2:2).

Repentance and the Restoration of the Divine Presence

The necessity of repentance underscores that salvation and redemption of humanity is the restoration of the divine Presence. Rebellion is an intentional move away from God's Presence. Repentance, then, is the deliberate move back to God's Presence. The Holy Spirit empowers repentance for the sake of restoring the Presence of God.

The call to repentance is synonymous with Jesus's invitation for people to come to him. He says:

- "*Come to me*, all who labor and are heavy laden, and I will give you rest"[10] (Matt. 11:28, italics added).
- "I am the bread of life; *whoever comes to me* shall not hunger, and whoever believes in me shall never thirst" (John 6:35, italics added).

---

10. Cf. Luke 6:47

- "All that the Father gives to me *will come to me*, and whoever comes to me I will never cast out" (John 6:37, italics added).
- "If anyone thirsts, let him *come to me* and drink" (John 7:37b, italics added).

Repentance is an intentional *going to Jesus's presence* by the enablement of the Holy Spirit (John 5:37–43). Jesus tells the Pharisees that they do not recognize his voice because the Word does not abide in them. They cannot repent on their own in their fallenness and deception. Furthermore, in not recognizing Jesus's voice, they "refuse to come" (John 5:40) to him and do not receive him. Here in John 5, we find yet again that repentance is required for salvation ("that you may have life" [v.40]) and Spirit-enabled.

Justifying Faith: The Holy Spirit's Gift

While Holy Spirit–enabled repentance is required for salvation, repentance does not provide a remedy for the disease of sin. As Athanasius puts it: "But repentance cannot avert the execution of a law; still less can it remedy a fallen nature."[11] The only remedy for the disease of sin is the pardon for

---

11. Athanasius of Alexandria, "On the Incarnation of the Word," in *St. Athanasius: Select Works and Letters* (New York: Christian Literature Company, 1892), 39.

sin-guilt through the atoning work of Jesus Christ. Only Jesus can restore us to favor with God.

Defining Justification

Justification, in the simplest sense, is pardon for sin-guilt. Guilt and punishment are the consequences of rebellion against God. The punishment for sin is ultimately death (Gen. 2:17; Matt. 25:46; John 3:16; Mark 9:43; Rom. 5:12; 6:23; 2 Thess. 1:9).

> Justification is ultimately about the restoration of his divine Presence through the Holy Spirit.

Death is the natural consequence of sin because sin separates us from God, who is the giver of life (Isa. 59:2). On the merits of Christ's perfect obedience and substitutionary death, and through the grace-enabled justifying faith of the believer, God declares the guilty sinner innocent. By doing so, God makes the sinner righteous, or just.[12]

---

12. For various views on the doctrine of justification, see N. T. Wright, *Justification: God's Plan, Paul's Vision* (London: SPCK, 2009); Paul Rhodes et al., *Justification: Five Views* (Downers Grove, IL: IVP Academic, 2011); and Mark Husbands and Daniel J. Trier, *Justification: What's at Stake in the Current Debates* (Downers Grove, IL: InterVarsity Press, 2004).

Atonement

Since the problem of sin is the loss of the Presence of God, justification is ultimately about the restoration of his divine Presence through the Holy Spirit. Justification is the means for the reconciliation between God and humanity. This reconciliation between God and us is the basis of the term "atonement" (i.e., "at-one-ment"), which is at the heart of justification. Atonement describes what justification accomplishes: restoring a ruptured divine-human relationship, making those who were at odds "at one." Justification draws on the imagery of a courtroom in which God judges and declares us—the guilty—innocent based on Christ's sacrifice on our behalf.

Justification as the declaration of innocence reaches beyond the courtroom metaphor in Scripture. Family relationship dynamics are also a vital part of the biblical notion of atonement. Atonement means that we, who were once estranged members of God's family, are brought back into a peaceful and loving relationship with the one who made us in his image; the one who made us members of the divine family (John 1:12–13; Rom. 8:15–17). Atonement, then, is much more about reconciliation than it is about the simple declaration of innocence. This becomes clearer when

> Atonement is much more about reconciliation than it is about the simple declaration of innocence.

we consider two key concepts at the heart of the biblical notion of atonement: (1) propitiation and (2) expiation.

Propitiation is the appeasement of God's wrath incurred against us when we rebel against him. Jumping off a two-story building would break your legs. Having broken legs means experiencing the wrath of the laws of physics. Defying God has consequences too. When we rebel against him, we throw ourselves against the moral laws of the universe and become bruised, battered, broken, and ultimately die as a result. This is exactly what Isaiah is describing when he says:

> Why will you still be struck down?
> > Why will you continue to rebel?
> The whole head is sick,
> > and the whole heart faint.
> From the sole of the foot even to the head,
> > there is no soundness in it,
> but bruises and sores
> > and raw wounds;
> they are not pressed out or bound up
> > or softened with oil. (1:5–6)

Jesus, the innocent one, willingly takes on the punishment that we deserve. He absorbs God's wrath into himself through his public shaming and crucifixion. This is the idea at the center of Isaiah's famous Suffering Servant song, a portion of which says:

> Surely he has borne our griefs
>   and carried our sorrows;
> yet we esteemed him stricken,
>   smitten by God, and afflicted.
> But he was pierced for our transgressions;
>   he was crushed for our iniquities;
> *upon him was the chastisement that brought us peace,*
>   *and with his wounds we are healed.*
> All we like sheep have gone astray;
>   we have turned—every one—to his own way;
> and the Lord has laid on him
>   the iniquity of us all. (53:4–6, italics added)

Jesus took on our griefs and carried away our sorrows, yours and mine. He did this so that God's wrath would turn away from us so that we could be reconciled to him and have peace with God. With God's wrath neutralized through the cross, fellowship between God and us is possible. That fellowship, says Isaiah, brings healing.

> Yes, we are all victims of sin, but principally, we are rebels against God.

There is a popular notion that sinners are merely victims and not criminals. The Scripture refutes this idea. It fails to acknowledge the Scripture-wide theme of God's wrath against sin (Rom. 2:5, 8; 13:4–5; Eph. 5:6). While Scripture affirms that living in a broken world means that we are all victims and that the gospel has a therapeutic dynamic, that reality is only one side of the coin. Yes, we are victims, but principally, we are rebels against God. We are not merely sinners who have caught the disease of sin and "languish in a sickbed as the Great Physician nurtures [us] on to *degrees* of health and wholeness."[13] Far from it. We are perpetrators "who not only actively [feed our] own inbred sinful inclination to depart from the living God, but also [are] quite energetic in [our] opposition, even rebellion, against a God of holy love."[14]

As guilty sinners, we need to be cleansed from our sin-guilt, which is what expiation accomplishes. Expiation wipes the criminal record clean. According to the Scriptures, sin makes us "unclean" (Lev. 5:2–3). John writes: "If we confess our sins, he is faithful and just to forgive us our sins and to cleanse us from all unrighteousness" (1 John 1:9). The blood of Christ is the means of cleansing for sin-guilt. Paul writes: "Since, therefore, we have now been justified by his blood, much more shall we be saved by him from the wrath of God" (Rom. 5:9). As the perfect and innocent sacrificial lamb of God, Jesus washes sinners from their guilt by taking sin-guilt into himself at the cross. Because of Jesus, sinners can be made clean (Isa. 52:13–53:12).

The divine-human relationship can be restored with the wrath of God appeased and sin-guilt cleansed. Those who

---

13. Kenneth J. Collins, *The Theology of John Wesley: Holy Love and the Shape of Grace* (Nashville: Abingdon Press, 2011), 106, italics in original.

14. Collins, 106.

were once estranged from one another can be brought back to a love relationship on the merits of Christ.

But if Christ is the primary actor in making atonement possible, where does the Holy Spirit come into the doctrine of justification? We will explore in the following sections how the gift of faith activates justification and that the Holy Spirit is the one who inspires that faith that applies the cleansing blood of Jesus in our lives.

Justification by Faith

We can have right standing before God on the merits of Christ's obedience by grace through faith. Freedom from the guilt of sin is not something that we earn; it is a gift of the Holy Spirit that we receive by faith. Paul writes: "For we hold that one is *justified by faith* apart from works of the law" (Rom. 3:28, italics added). He explains further, saying: "Yet we know that a person is not justified by works of the law *but through faith in Jesus Christ*, so we also have believed in Christ Jesus, to be *justified by faith* in Christ and not by works of the law, because by works of the law no one will be justified" (Gal. 2:16, italics added).

Genesis 15 gives us a clear example of justifying faith. In this story, God promises a sterile Abraham and Sarah the

> The only way we can fully trust in the unbelievable claims of the gospel is with help from the supernatural.

impossible: innumerable offspring. Abraham believed in God. He trusted God. He had confidence that God would make good on this promise. As the apostle Paul famously underscores, it was Abraham's trust in God to accomplish the impossible that rendered him righteous (Rom. 4:13). Abraham's faith was trust in God over and above empirical confidence in facts. Even belief in the historical facts of the inspired Scripture and doctrinal declarations is ultimately trusting in the trustworthy, omniscient God, for even the demons believe in the facts (James 2:19).

The only way we can fully trust in the unbelievable claims of the gospel is with help from the supernatural. Consider all the miraculous things that Christians affirm; things like the virgin birth, bodily resurrection, and that Jesus is fully God. Add to this list events in Scripture like the Red Sea crossing, the resurrection of Lazarus, Jesus walking on water and calming the storm. We also affirm belief in angels, demons, and Satan. It takes faith to believe these things. It takes the ability to say, "I don't know *how* it's true, but I believe *that* it's true." The ability to believe is given to us

> The Holy Spirit makes it possible for us to believe in the miraculous claim that God can love and transform sinners like you and me.

by the Holy Spirit because of grace. We struggle to believe. Our tendency, especially Westerners, is to doubt anything that is not provable or measurable. If it can't be explained by nature and reason, doubt it. That's the message that we are raised with and surrounds us. That's why we need the Holy Spirit to help us believe. The Holy Spirit makes it possible for us to believe in the miraculous claim that God can love and transform sinners like you and me.

But what kind of faith does the Holy Spirit give us? He provides us unwavering faith. The faith that the Holy Spirit puts in our hearts is stalwart, strong, and perfect. Holy Spirit–faith casts mountains into seas and turns sinners into saints. The Holy Spirit is the breath that sustains our faith in Jesus and his works. Greater is the Holy Spirit in us than the one who whispers, "God is not trustworthy, doesn't love you, and can't forgive you." The Holy Spirit shares his loyalty to God the Father and God the Son with us. By the Holy Spirit, we can believe that Jesus is the divine Son (1 Cor. 12:3).

> The Holy Spirit shares his loyalty to God the Father and God the Son with us.

Trusting faith is essential to the way of salvation because distrust and suspicion are at the heart of our estrangement from God. Faith is the restoration of that trust necessary for a love relationship. The Deceiver tempted Adam and Eve to believe that God was neither trustworthy nor loving. By grace, the love of God in the cross counters this lie. Faith is belief in the truth of God's love and trustworthiness over the lie of the Murderer. Hope empowered by grace compels a move toward God to ask for forgiveness for not trusting him and for rebelling against him. As Ambrose put it so succinctly: "Faith asks for forgiveness."[15] The Holy Spirit, by grace, empowers that kind of faith.

Pardon for sin-guilt (i.e., justification) is only actualized with the accompanying work of the Holy Spirit to inspire faith in sinners to receive the gift that God offers us in Christ. This is the role of the Holy Spirit in justification. We are left dead in our sins without the Holy Spirit actively inspiring our faith in Christ and his merits. The Holy Spirit inspires in us a faith in the fact that Christ died not only for the world, but for me, and takes away even my sins. It is a faith that is accompanied by an assurance that we are dead in sin, and alive in Christ.

Regeneration: The Holy Spirit Gives Life

Regeneration, which is at the heart of scriptural conversion, is the new birth that occurs when we receive the Holy Spirit (more on Spirit baptism in the next section). The move from justification to regeneration goes from what God does for us (justification) to what God does in us (regeneration). With justification comes the deliverance from the guilt of sin. With regeneration comes freedom from the power of

---

15. Ambrose of Milan, "Two Books Concerning Repentance," in *St. Ambrose: Select Works and Letters* (New York: Christian Literature Company, 1896), 355.

sin. Thomas Oden writes: "In justification a new relation with God is juridically declared. In regeneration, new life is given that bestows and embodies that new relationship. Justification refers to a change in one's standing before God; regeneration, to a new beginning of a life that manifests that new standing."[16]

Many Christians think about salvation too narrowly by thinking in terms of what God does for us in declaring us innocent. However, God's plan of salvation does not stop at changing the status of sinners from guilty to innocent. Far from it. His plan, instead, is to redeem his original purpose for humanity to be his faithful image-bearers. This is only possible through the radical healing of human nature. That healing begins with new birth. To be a Christian, as Paul puts it, is to be a new creation. He writes: "Therefore, if anyone is in Christ, he is a new creation. The old has passed away; behold, the new has come" (2 Cor. 5:17). Christians were once dead in their sin but are now alive in Christ (Eph. 2:4–5).[17]

In the new birth, God breaks the power of canceled sin. It is freedom from the power of sinning. Faith, hope, and

---

16. Oden, *Life in the Spirit*, 158.
17. See also Colossians 3:10 and Ephesians 2:15.

love—the marks of the new birth—overthrow the despotic reign of the sin in our hearts. As John puts it: "No one who is born of God practices sin, because his seed abides in him; he cannot sin, because he is born of God" (1 John 3:9 NASB). Paul develops this idea by writing:

> What shall we say then? Are we to continue in sin that grace may abound? By no means! How can we who died to sin still live in it? Do you not know that all of us who have been baptized into Christ Jesus were baptized into his death? We were buried therefore with him by baptism into death, in order that, just as Christ was raised from the dead by the glory of the Father, we too might walk in newness of life.
>
> For if we have been united with him in a death like his, we shall certainly be united with him in a resurrection like his. We know that our old self was crucified with him in order that the body of sin might be brought to nothing, so that we would no longer be enslaved to sin. For one who has died has been set free from sin. Now if we have died with Christ, we believe that we will also live with him. We know that Christ, being raised from the dead, will never die again; death no longer has dominion over him. For the death he died he died to sin, once for all, but the life he lives he lives to God. So you also must consider yourselves dead to sin and alive to God in Christ Jesus. (Rom. 6:1–11)

The Scriptures plainly reveal that regeneration is the work of the Holy Spirit. Paul says in Titus 3:5: "He saved us, not on the basis of deeds which we have done in righteousness, but according to his mercy, by the washing of *regeneration* and renewing *by the Holy Spirit*" (NASB, italics added). The Christian is the one who is born of the Spirit into a new life in Christ. Jesus tells Nicodemus: "Truly, truly I say to you, unless one is born of the water and Spirit, he cannot enter the kingdom of God. That which is born of the flesh is flesh, and that which is born of the Spirit is spirit" (John 3:5–6).[18]

In Genesis 1:2, the Holy Spirit hovered over the darkness and chaos to bring light and life into the world. The same Holy Spirit hovers over the darkness and chaos of the human condition to bring light and life as God originally intended. In Psalm 51:10, David makes an appeal to God, saying, "Create in me a clean heart, O God, and renew a right spirit within me." The Hebrew verb translated "create" here is *bara*. God is only ever the subject of the verb *bara* in the Old Testament. It is also the same verb in Genesis 1:1 when it says: "In the beginning God created the

> The same Holy Spirit hovers over the darkness and chaos of the human condition to bring light and life as God originally intended.

---

18. See also John 1:12–13; 6:63; 1 John 5:1.

heavens and the earth." David is asking God to do that which only God can do, and that is to recreate his heart. David is saying to God, "It's not my actions that are the problem; it's my very nature! Change my nature!" God created humanity once. He can certainly do it again.

> "It's not my actions that are the problem; it's my very nature! Change my nature!"

We gain a clear vision of the regenerating ministry of the Holy Spirit in Ezekiel's vision of the valley of dry bones in Ezekiel 37. The Holy Spirit led the prophet to a valley of human bones. The Spirit then instructed Ezekiel to prophesy over the bones, which he did. The bones then took on flesh but were not yet living. God then breathes on the bodies, and they come to life, as a great army. In this vision, God has the power to recreate a community, and how he does that is by the Holy Spirit.

In John 20:22, Jesus breathes on his disciples and says, "Receive the Holy Spirit." This reenactment of the creation of Adam in Genesis 2:2 demonstrates Christ-followers as members of the new creation race of humans in Jesus (more on this in the section on the Holy Spirit and the church). This is the life-regenerating work of the Spirit of Life. John Wesley identifies the marks of the new birth as faith, hope, and love, all of which are a radical departure from the marks of the old nature of the flesh and only possible through the empowerment of the Holy Spirit. Wesley writes:

This it is, in the judgment of the Spirit of God, to be a son or a child of God. It is so to believe in God through Christ as "not to commit sin", and to enjoy, at all times and in all places, that "peace of God which passeth all understanding". It is so to *hope* in God through the Son of his love as to have not only the "testimony of a good conscience", but also "the Spirit of God bearing witness with your spirits that ye are the children of God": whence cannot but spring the "rejoicing evermore in him through whom ye have received the atonement". It is so to *love* God, who hath thus loved you, as you never did love any creature: so that ye are constrained to love all men as yourselves; with a love not only ever burning in your hearts, but flaming out in all your actions and conversations, and making your whole life one "labour of love", one continued obedience to those commands, "Be ye merciful, as God is merciful;" "Be ye holy, as I the Lord am holy;" "Be ye perfect, as your Father which is in heaven is perfect."[19]

---

19. John Wesley, "The Marks of the New Birth," in *The Sermons of John Wesley: A Collection for the Christian Journey*, eds. Kenneth J. Collins and Jason E. Vickers (Nashville: Abingdon Press, 2013), 172.

Baptism of the Holy Spirit

Baptism of the Holy Spirit occurs when the Holy Spirit takes up residence in believers and breaks the power of canceled sin. Spirit baptism fulfills God's promise to make the human heart his home. It is the restoration of the divine Presence lost at the fall in Genesis 3. The restoration of the divine Presence is therapeutic to the corrupted and diseased human nature. The healing it brings restores the holy-love character attributes to humanity that God always intended to share with his image-bearers. In other words, the baptism of the Holy Spirit makes people fully human; Spirit baptism makes people look like Jesus.

> The baptism of the Holy Spirit makes people fully human; Spirit baptism makes people look like Jesus.

The Old Testament Promises Spirit Baptism

The Old Testament prophets predicted Spirit baptism. Jeremiah describes the restoration and renewal of the human nature that will come with this new covenant as the law of God being written on the hearts of his people:

> "Behold, the days are coming, declares the LORD, when I will make a new covenant with the house of Israel and the house of Judah, not like the covenant

> that I made with their fathers. . . . For this is the covenant that I will make with the house of Israel after those days, declares the Lord: I will put my law within them, and I will write it on their hearts. And I will be their God, and they shall be my people." (Jer. 31:31–33)

The law of God is a picture of who God is. His holy love is embedded in his commands for his image-bearers. For his law to be transcribed on hearts is a metaphor meaning that God's people will be the embodiment of his holy love; they will be bearers of his image as he always intended.

In the tradition of David in Psalm 51:10–11, Ezekiel describes this same dynamic as God giving his people a new heart and a new Spirit. He says:

> "I will take you from the nations and gather you from all the countries and bring you into your own land. I will sprinkle clean water on you, and you shall be clean from all your uncleannesses, and from all your idols I will cleanse you. *And I will give you a new heart, and a new spirit I will put within you. And I will remove the heart of stone from your flesh and give you a heart of flesh. And I will put my Spirit within you,* and cause you to walk in my statutes and be careful to obey my rules. You shall dwell in the land that I gave to your fathers, and you shall be my people, and I will be your God." (Ezek. 36:24–28, italics added)

Daniel Block helpfully points out that:

> [The heart] represents the person's internal locus of emotion, will, and thought. Like Jesus, centuries later (Matt. 15:17–20), Ezekiel recognized the problem of rebellion and sin against Yahweh to be more deeply ingrained than mere external acts. Ezekiel concretizes the metaphor by describing the heart as *stone*, which speaks of coldness, insensitivity, incorrigibility, and even lifelessness (cf. 1 Sam. 25:37).[20]

However, the new Spirit that God will give Israel in this new covenant will be different from the first in two respects. First, God specifies that he will put his Spirit within believers. Second, the prophecy foretells that this new spirit will be "my [Yahweh's] Spirit." In sum, this new heart and new spirit will create a new humanity that will be faithful to the divine-image-bearing vocation.

The prophet Joel also foretells of the pouring out of the Spirit:

> And it shall come to pass afterward, that I will pour out my Spirit on all flesh; your sons and your

---

20. Daniel I. Block, *The Book of Ezekiel: Chapters 25–48*, The New International Commentary on the Old Testament (Grand Rapids: Eerdmans, 1998), 355, italics added.

daughters shall prophesy, your old men shall dream dreams, and your young men shall see visions. Even on the male and female servants in those days I will pour out my Spirit. (Joel 2:28–29)

Two noteworthy things here. First, the prophet emphasizes that the Spirit of Yahweh will be poured out on *all flesh*, which is distinct from the norms of the first covenant. Second, and in harmony with Ezekiel, the Spirit that will be poured out is the Spirit of Yahweh himself.

This new Spirit-covenant would accomplish what the Mosaic law could not accomplish: a *transformation of human nature*. The Mosaic law made provision for the external cleansing of sin-guilt. The new covenant would make provision for internal cleansing.

Jesus and John Promise Spirit Baptism

John the Baptist explained that while he baptized with water, Jesus would baptize with the Holy Spirit and fire (Matt. 3:11). Even Jesus himself taught that he would pour out the Holy Spirit on his followers (John 14:15–17). The disciples were often either utterly surprised by or confused at what Jesus taught them, including the need for his substitutionary death (Matt. 16:22). The baptism of the Holy Spirit, however, was never questioned by the disciples. They understood and even expected this teaching from Jesus because of the promises of the Old Testament prophets.

Pentecost: The Fulfillment of the Promise

In his Pentecost sermon, Peter explained to the crowd that this promise of the Old Testament prophets, John the Baptist, and Jesus was fulfilled on that day. While many were confused at what was happening at the Pentecost event, Peter explained. He says: "Being therefore exalted at the right hand of God, and having received from the Father the promise of the Holy Spirit, he has poured out this that you yourselves are seeing and hearing" (Acts 2:33). Peter understood that the prophecy was fulfilled at Pentecost because Jesus told them of the new covenant during the Last Supper.

> Jesus's followers understood and even expected this baptism of the Holy Spirit because of the promises of the Old Testament prophets.

Is Spirit Baptism Distinct from New Birth Regeneration?

When Holy Spirit baptism occurs is debated across various traditions. Most traditions affirm that baptism of the Holy Spirit is simultaneous with the new birth, hence the language of being "born of the Spirit" (John 3:5) that results from justifying faith. Other traditions posit that Spirit baptism is a "second work of grace" after regeneration and the result of the Christian's response to a deeper work of the Holy Spirit.

While both views find support in Scripture, most agree that the expected norm of the apostles in various scenarios in the book of Acts is for Spirit baptism to occur in the moment of conversion and that accounts of a Spirit baptism occurring after justifying faith are abnormal.

However, is it possible that those abnormal scenarios could happen again and be widespread in a time and place in which only a partial gospel is preached? The Samaritans in Acts 8:14–17, for example, had not received the Spirit because they were not taught about the Spirit from the start. Could that happen again in Christian communities today, or was that a one-off anomaly? While the disciples' Spirit baptism at Pentecost occurred subsequently to their justifying faith in Jesus, it is easier to see how their situation was a unique, unrepeatable scenario (i.e., having lived through the historical events that gave birth to the church). That the case of the Samaritans would be a one-off situation is not as obvious. It seems feasible that while Spirit baptism at the time of conversion is the norm in Scripture, there could be scenarios where a lack of teaching of the whole gospel could result in the necessity of Spirit baptism after conversion.

Nonetheless, John Wesley's view of Spirit baptism is helpful here. Wesley understood the sinful condition as

> The expected norm of the apostles in various scenarios in the book of Acts is for Spirit baptism to occur in the moment of conversion.

an inheritance of infirmity due to the loss of the divine Presence (i.e., Holy Spirit) at the fall. The work of Jesus, which is not just to forgive but to restore, gives back to humanity what was lost.

Against this understanding of the human condition and its causes, the new birth is the initial baptism in the Holy Spirit, the moment that the individual receives the gift of the Holy Spirit to recreate human life (John 3:1–8). The emphasis here is that Jesus came to restore what was lost in Adam's rebellion: the divine Presence. The restoration of the divine Presence *via* the Holy Spirit then sets the Christian on a trajectory to experience a fullness of this baptism, which is a subsequent matter. Experiencing the fullness of the Spirit baptism is subsequent because the formation into desiring the fullness of the Spirit is essential for personal responsiveness to God and a personal yielding to more of God's work in the believer's life.

> The work of Jesus, which is not just to forgive but to restore, gives back to humanity what was lost.

There is a clear distinction, then, between the recreating gift of the Holy Spirit in the new birth and the subsequent encounter in the life of discipleship where one's life is consciously and fully yielded to the transforming Presence and lordship of the Holy Spirit. This is a gradual dying to self, by the empowerment of the Holy Spirit, which enables the believer to experience all the Spirit's fullness.

Sanctification: The Spirit of Christ

Sanctification is the ongoing process of the Holy Spirit shaping the child of God into the likeness of Christ. The image of God restored in us is the fruit of the Holy Spirit coming home to the human heart. Regeneration is the initial step of deliverance from the power of sin. Sanctification is the necessary and natural next step in the image-restoring process. In sanctification, the Holy Spirit attacks the root of sin in our lives and shapes and forms in us holy habits and desires. Justification and regeneration free the believer from the guilt and power of sin. Sanctification, on the other hand, frees us to love God and others. It is, as John Wesley put it, "love excluding sin; love filling the heart, taking up the whole capacity of the soul. It is love 'rejoicing evermore, praying without ceasing, in everything giving thanks.'"[21]

The Holy Spirit Sanctifies

While sanctification is the fruit of the Holy Spirit restoring the divine Presence in our lives, the Holy Spirit is also the active agent in sanctifying us. Paul says, "But we ought always to give thanks to God for you, brothers beloved by the

---

21. John Wesley, "The Scripture Way of Salvation" in *The Sermons of John Wesley: A Collection for the Christian Journey*, eds. Kenneth J. Collins and Jason E. Vickers (Nashville: Abingdon Press, 2013), 585.

Lord, because God chose you as the firstfruits to be saved, *through sanctification by the Spirit* and belief in the truth" (2 Thess. 2:13, italics added). It is by the Spirit that we're sanctified. Peter says that sanctification is *of the Spirit*. He writes: "according to the foreknowledge of God the Father, *in the sanctification of the Spirit*, for obedience to Jesus Christ and for sprinkling with his blood: May grace and peace be multiplied to you" (1 Peter 1:2, italics added).[22]

Freedom from Sin, Freedom to Obey

Peter points out in the 1 Peter 1:2 that sanctification is for the purpose of obedience to Christ. The freedom in Christ that comes with sanctification is freedom from sin and sinning and freedom to obey God in righteousness. Paul writes: "I am speaking in human terms, because of your natural limitations. For just as you once presented your members as slaves to impurity and to lawlessness leading to more lawlessness, so now present your members as slaves to righteousness leading to sanctification" (Rom. 6:19). He goes on to say: "But now that you have been set free from sin and have become

> The freedom in Christ that comes with sanctification is freedom from sin and sinning and freedom to obey God in righteousness.

---

22. See also Romans 15:16.

slaves of God, the fruit you get leads to sanctification and its end, eternal life" (Rom. 6:22).[23]

Sanctification

In proceeding, we will divide sanctification into three parts: (1) initial sanctification, (2) gradual sanctification, and (3) entire sanctification.

Initial Sanctification

Initial sanctification, which happens simultaneously with regeneration, is the initial liberation from the power of sin. Initial sanctification is an instantaneous work that the Holy Spirit does in us on his own. Initial sanctification also entails a measure of assurance of salvation. This is distinct from the full assurance of salvation which comes with entire sanctification (more following). The measured assurance that comes with initial sanctification is an assurance that experiences occasional doubt and fear. These doubts and fears are not the results of being subject to the dominion of

> Entire sanctification is the fullness of the Spirit, victory over sin, and a life of holy love.

---

23. See also 1 Corinthians 1:30.

sin but of years of sinful habits that are the fruit of sin being embedded in us.

Gradual Sanctification

Gradual sanctification is the process of the Holy Spirit's attacking of the root of sin. It is the Holy Spirit leading us in dying to self. It is the gradual straightening of the inward bent. It is the healing of human nature that is diseased by sin. It is the process of the restoration of the image of God in us.

Gradual sanctification is distinct from initial sanctification in several ways:

1. In gradual sanctification, the Holy Spirit works with us as he uproots the cause of sin. Grace empowers our participation and is therefore utterly dependent on God. This is different than initial sanctification. Initial sanctification is something the Holy Spirit accomplishes free from our participation.
2. Gradual sanctification is ongoing, while initial sanctification is instantaneous.
3. Gradual sanctification increases the measure of assurance of salvation that is given at initial sanctification.

Creating holy habits and the deeper cleansing from the root of sin further frees us from doubt and fear. In gradual sanctification, the Holy Spirit shows us the parts of our lives that we have yet to yield to him.

Entire Sanctification

Entire sanctification is the fullness of the Spirit, victory over sin, and a life of holy love. By fullness of the Spirit, we mean the state in which the Holy Spirit gets all of us; it means we have the Spirit in every part of us. We have given ourselves over entirely for the Holy Spirit to move freely in us and through us. Entire sanctification is the work of the Holy Spirit in perfecting our love of God and neighbor by making that holy love our highest desire.

Positive and Negative Aspects of Entire Sanctification

This perfect love for God and neighbor Wesley called "Christian perfection," which he defines as:

> A full salvation from all our sins, from pride, self-will, anger, unbelief, or, as the Apostle expresses it, "Go on to perfection" [Heb. 6:1 KJV]. But what is perfection? The word has various senses: here it means perfect love. It is love excluding sin; love filling the heart, taking up the whole capacity of the soul. It is love "rejoicing evermore, praying

without ceasing, in everything giving thanks" [1 Thess. 5:16–18 KJV].[24]

According to Wesley, we can think of entire sanctification both negatively and positively. Negatively, entire sanctification is the elimination of sin from our nature. It is the total correction of our inward bent toward self. Positively, entire sanctification is the freedom to have an undivided heart that is singularly fixed on loving and obeying God; it means experiencing the fullness of God's perfect love.

> Positively, entire sanctification is the freedom to have an undivided heart that is singularly fixed on loving and obeying God.

The Work of God, Not Human Accomplishment

The claim that Christians can be made perfect in love seems like a tall order. Still, perfection in love is both the mandatory and natural follow-up of regeneration because if for no other reason than that he who begins a good work sees it through to completion (Phil. 1:6). The promise of entire sanctification is not a claim to what we are capable of but of what the sovereign holy Trinity can accomplish in sinners. Christian perfection is the fruit of belief that the redemptive

---

24. John Wesley, "The Scripture Way of Salvation," 585.

work of the Father, the Son, and the Holy Spirit is powerful enough to transform self-centered sinners into individuals who are fully abandoned to God. It is as Paul says: "Now may the God of peace himself *sanctify you completely*, and may your whole spirit and soul and body be kept blameless at the coming of our Lord Jesus Christ. *He who calls you is faithful; he will surely do it*" (1 Thess. 5:23–24, italics added).

Pleasing God Is the Highest Desire

The doctrine of entire sanctification affirms the biblical teaching that Christians need not sin. We need not sin because the Holy Spirit has dealt with the cause of sinning, which the apostle Paul calls the "flesh" (Rom. 7–8). Habitual sin results from a willful determination to have our way in life. As we've been discussing all along, the Holy Spirit can transform this pattern of thinking and acting. The Holy Spirit can make it so that pleasing God is our highest desire. Because of the Holy Spirit, we can have what the Bible calls a "whole heart."[25] This is not a heart that is flawless in all its understandings, or even in all its feelings, but one that is completely given over to

> Because of the Holy Spirit, we can have what the Bible calls a "whole heart."

---

25. See e.g., 1 Kings 15:14 (KJV) "perfect heart." Modern translations struggle to avoid the connotations of flawlessness that "perfect" conveys.

knowing and serving God.[26] The result is that a person is no longer inclined or "bent" to disobeying but is now "bent" to please God.

The Indwelling of Perfect Love

Being filled with the Holy Spirit is synonymous with the fullness of perfect, holy love. The Holy Spirit is the gift of the Father and the Son to the world. When the Father and Son send the Holy Spirit to indwell believers, it is the indwelling of a holy love free from deficiency or corruption. Entire sanctification is the witness of God's promise to extend the perfect bond of holy fellowship with Christians; it is the embodiment of being given over entirely to the perfect love of God that is the Holy Spirit.

> Christ can command that Christians be perfected in love because the Holy Spirit is the source of that love.

Jesus can declare that Christian righteousness must exceed that of the Pharisees on the basis of his own perfect righteousness that is transferred to the believer (Matt. 5:20; 2 Cor. 5:21).[27] Similarly, Christ can

---

26. Wesley specified that entire sanctification does not include being perfect in knowledge, free from mistakes, free from infirmities, free from temptation, nor free from further growth.

27. See also Isaiah 46:13; 51:5; 56:1; Romans 1:17; 3:22; 1 Corinthians 1:30.

command that Christians be perfected in love because the Holy Spirit, the gift that is the bond of perfect and holy love between the Father and the Son, is the source of that love (Matt. 5:48).

Full Assurance of Salvation and the Witness of the Spirit

We said that assurance of salvation in initial and gradual sanctification is measured. In entire sanctification, we experience the full assurance of salvation, or what Wesley calls the witness of the Spirit. The witness of the Spirit is the Holy Spirit assuring us of being reconciled to God. It is free from doubt and fear. On the one hand, there is the witness of our own spirit that we are children of God. We know that if we bear the fruit of the Spirit, have a clean conscience, and obey God, then we can be sure that we are in Christ. Wesley called this the "indirect witness." It is the witness of holy love; love for God, neighbors, and even enemies. It is a supernatural love beyond the corrupt human imagination and the Devil's delusions. It must be a love that originates within the inner life of the holy Trinity. When we see it in ourselves, we can be certain that God has redeemed us.

On the other hand, there is a different kind of witness directly from the Holy Spirit. This witness is different than simply observing the fruit of the Spirit in our own lives.

This is what Wesley called the direct witness and describes it this way:

> By "the testimony of the Spirit" I mean an inward impression of the soul, whereby the Spirit of God immediately and directly witnesses to my spirit that I am a child of God, that Jesus Christ hath loved me, and given himself for me; that all my sins are blotted out, and I, even I, am reconciled to God . . . The Spirit of God does give a believer such a testimony of his adoption that while it is present to the soul he can no more doubt the reality of his sonship that he can doubt of the shining of the sun while he stands in the full blaze of his beams.[28]

Wesley points out that the Spirit's witness of the lordship of Christ is linked to the Spirit's testimony to the adoption of the believer into the family of God (Gal. 4:6). The Spirit affirms *directly to the believer* that they are saved. It is as Paul says: "The Spirit himself testifies with our spirit that we are the children of God" (Rom. 8:16).

---

28. John Wesley, "The Witness of the Spirit, I," in *The Sermons of John Wesley: A Collection for the Christian Journey*, eds. Kenneth J. Collins and Jason E. Vickers (Nashville: Abingdon Press, 2013), 199–200.

Sanctified in Christ by the Holy Spirit and Inner Cleansing

Sanctification is the work of the Holy Spirit based on the merits of Christ's atoning work. It is clear from the Old Testament—especially Leviticus—that atonement sanctifies. The word *sanctify* and its derivatives appear eighteen times in the Old Testament. Ten of those eighteen occurrences appear in the context of some form of the phrase, "I am the Lord who sanctifies you." Seven of those ten occurrences are in Leviticus and located in contexts treating the sacrificial system and atonement. As we discussed in the previous sections, atonement cleanses the sinner of sin-guilt. This cleansing, then, sanctifies. It makes clean by changing the sinner's status from guilty to innocent.

> Sanctification is the work of the Holy Spirit based on the merits of Christ's atoning work.

The sacrificial system of the Old Testament had the power to sanctify externally. In the New Testament covenant, however, Jesus provides a means for internal cleansing, which is a metaphor for transforming our nature or removing the root of sinning. We get this point from the story of the wedding of Cana in John 2. In that story, Jesus turns water into wine. The water was in Jewish stone purification jars. That means that these stone jars would hold water used for ceremonial and/or ritual cleansing. We learn from another story of the Gospels that Jews would have to wash their hands before eating (Luke 11:38). They would wash using special water (think holy water) held in these jars. The water that came from these jars makes one holy or clean. When Jesus turns the water in these jars to wine to drink, it is an image of internal cleansing. Washing with water from these jars cleans the outside, and sipping wine from these jars cleanses the inside. Without going into great detail, there are other elements of this story that indicate that John is telling us that Jesus has come to institute a new covenant that would be better than the old covenant. There was provision for external cleansing in the first covenant, meaning forgiveness for sins that we commit. However, in the new Jesus covenant, there is provision for internal cleansing, meaning the purging of the cause of sinning.

> Our big problem is not that we commit sins, it's that we have inherited an inward bent, which makes it impossible not to sin.

Our big problem is not that we commit sins, it's that we have inherited an inward bent, which makes it impossible not to sin. The first covenant makes provision to forgive us of the sins we commit, but it does not have the power to purge the disease of sin from our hearts. This is where Jesus, the new covenant, and the Holy Spirit come in. Jesus makes cleansing possible for the indwelling of the Holy Spirit to attack the root of sin. This story of the wine from the wedding of Cana makes it clear: Jesus makes it possible for us to be cleansed internally.

In sum, the indwelling of the holy fire of the Holy Spirit cleanses us of sin (Mark 1:7–8). The Holy Spirit purges the rebel heart of its bent toward sinning. The illuminating fire of the Holy Spirit reveals sin and cleanses the life of sin. This is a crucial difference between the Mosaic covenant of the Old Testament and the new covenant of the New Testament. Both reveal sin and corruption, but only in the new covenant does the Holy Spirit empower us to overcome sin. The Holy Spirit reveals the disease of sinful actions, attitudes, and thoughts so that he can purge them from the believer.

> The Holy Spirit purges the rebel heart of its bent toward sinning.

Glorification: The Holy Spirit Raises the Dead

Glorification takes salvation to full completion with the redemption of our physical bodies. The Holy Spirit glorified Jesus on the third day by raising him from the dead (Rom. 1:4). The Scriptures promise that those in Christ will also be raised from the dead. Paul writes: "If the Spirit of him who raised Jesus from the dead dwells in you, he who raised Christ Jesus from the dead will also give life to your mortal bodies through his Spirit who dwells in you" (Rom. 8:11). As Paul points out, those in Christ receive the promise of a resurrection (Luke 20:34–40; John 11:25; 1 Cor. 15:51–57; 2 Cor. 5:1–9). The indwelling of the Holy Spirit unites us to Christ (1 Cor. 6:17; 12:13; 1 John 4:13), making us members of Christ's body. Being united with Christ includes union with his glorification. As we will see in later sections, bodily resurrection is the final vindication of those who are in Christ.

While the nature of the glorified body remains in large part a mystery, we know that the glorified body will have the same form as our current bodies but be of a different substance. C. S. Lewis compared the glorified body to a river. The water flowing through a river today is different from that which flowed through that same place yesterday or even a year ago, but it's the same river. In this case, the water is the substance, and the river is the form: different water, same river. As far as we can tell from the Gospel stories of Jesus's glorified body, our bodies will be similar; recognizable with the same form but with a different substance.

> Bodily resurrection is the final vindication of those who are in Christ.

We receive our glorified bodies after the final judgment. When Jesus returns in triumph over his enemies, we will receive resurrected, glorified bodies. Once again, the Holy Spirit is the one who will recreate our bodies to be perfect, as God always intended.

Conclusion

The Holy Spirit applies the saving work of Jesus in our lives by transforming us into Christ's very image. He does this by getting us back into God's life-giving Presence. The restoration of the divine Presence means the restoration of the image of God in us. By applying Christ's redemptive work, the Holy Spirit makes people what God always intended people to be: his image-bearers, his children that resemble him. When the image of God is restored in you and me, peace returns to the creation.

Why It Matters

God can change people. We are not subject to fate or destiny. We are not limited to a life on repeat and enslavement to passions and desires that lead to our ruin. In salvation, God breaks into history and radically transforms us in every way. Spirit-empowered transformation is not just about the dos and do nots. It's about transforming our very thoughts, attitudes, and emotions. The Christian life is not about sin management until Christ's return. It's about changing what interests us, motivates us, drives us. It's the renewal of our passions. The perfect love of God brought to us by the Holy Spirit can fully cast out fear, anxiety, depression, and deception. The Holy Spirit sets

> The Christian life is not about sin management until Christ's return.

captives free from the vices of our fallen state. The Holy Spirit also sets us free from the fear and certainty of death. The Holy Spirit cleanses our hearts of the disease of sin.

Questions for Reflection and Discussion

1. What are the steps in the order of salvation?
2. What is prevenient grace and why is it necessary for salvation?
3. How is regeneration different from sanctification?
4. What are the three divisions within sanctification?
5. What is entire sanctification?

CHAPTER 7

The Holy Spirit and the Church

The previous chapter looked at the role of the Holy Spirit in the order of salvation as it applies to the individual. In this chapter, we will look at the work of the Holy Spirit within the collective body of believers. We will see that the Holy Spirit works for believers and in believers and works through the collective body of Christ for the advancement of the kingdom of God. Ultimately, salvation is about the restoration of the Presence of God with his people. Jesus makes that possible, and the Holy Spirit carries it out through personal indwelling. There is fruit that comes from that indwelling that builds toward the final consummation of the triune God's redemptive purposes.

Defining Church

The church (*ekklesia*) is "the totality of congregations of Christians." It is the collective body of those who confess that Jesus Christ is Lord (Matt. 16:18). The Holy Spirit, not flesh and blood, gives witness to that confession (Matt. 16:17; 1 Cor. 12:3). As such, "the Church is, in a phrase used by the Fathers, 'where the Spirit flourishes.'"[1]

Union with Christ, Subsisting Relations, and the Holy Spirit

The church only exists in restored relationship with the holy Trinity. The Holy Spirit, on the merits of Christ's work, restores what was lost in the fall: divine-human relationship. The restoration of this relationship *brings the church into existence*. Restored relationship with the Creator constitutes the very being of the church. Just as the Holy Spirit brought Jesus into the world, he also births the church, the body of Christ, into the world.

> Restored relationship with the Creator constitutes the very being of the church.

The Holy Spirit gave birth to the church at Pentecost by bringing the disciples into union with Christ. The Holy Spirit filled each disciple as he did

---

1. Catholic Church, *Catechism of the Catholic Church*, 2nd ed. (Washington, DC: United States Catholic Conference, 2000), 197.

the temple in the Old Testament. This time, however, the temple is the unified body of Christ. In the new covenant, God is not just near but within. Eden, the place of divine-human fellowship and unity, is now in the heart of each believer.

While the Holy Spirit indwells individuals, each is a part of one baptism, worshipping one Lord, making up one temple (Eph. 4:5). Like the inner life of the Trinity, there is a mutual indwelling (*perichoresis*) among believers with one another, and with Christ. There is no single Christian apart from the rest, and there is no collective apart from the individual. There is unity with distinction, diversity in oneness. Through the church, the body of believers, salvation comes to the individual, never apart from it. The salvation of one always originates in another.

> There is no church without the Holy Spirit because there is no union with Christ without the Holy Spirit.

All of this is because, in being united with Christ who was united to humanity through the incarnation, humanity is introduced into the inner life of God. That new race in Jesus is the church, and the Holy Spirit is the personal bond of love that joins them together in unity. There is no church without the Holy Spirit because there is no union with Christ without the Holy Spirit. Furthermore, there is no union of Christ with the human nature (i.e., incarnation) without the Holy Spirit.

The Church Is Everlasting

The gates of hell will not prevail against the church because the Holy Spirit, the giver of eternal life, is the one who constitutes the church. The Holy Spirit's resurrecting power in the church is greater than that of the Murderer (1 John 4:4). The Light of the world came into the darkness, and the darkness could not overcome it (John 1:4–5). Life that is imparted to the church is everlasting (John 3:15–16). It is everlasting because it is a life that originates in and is united to the everlasting triune God on the merits of the righteousness of Christ (Matt. 25:46).

Jesus tells the Samaritan woman at the well that "whoever drinks of the water that I will give him will never be thirsty again. The water that I will give him will become in him a spring of water welling up to eternal life" (John 4:14). In speaking on the day of the feast, Jesus says something very similar to the crowd: "If anyone thirsts, let him come to me and drink. Whoever believes in me, as the Scripture has said, 'Out of his heart will flow rivers of living water'" (John 7:37–38). In the next verse, John tells us that these rivers of living water that lead to eternal life symbolize the Holy Spirit. He writes: "Now this he said about the Spirit, whom those who believed in him were to receive, for as yet the Spirit had not been given, because Jesus was not yet glorified."[2]

---

2. See also Galatians 6:8.

The Spirit Nourishes the Church

These same episodes from John's Gospel further reveal that the Holy Spirit nourishes the church. Nourishment comes to the church through the Holy Spirit and through the church to the world, as demonstrated in Ezekiel's temple vision. One feature of the new temple is that water will flow out of it. Ezekiel 47:1–2 says:

> Then he brought me back to the door of the temple, and behold, water was issuing from below the threshold of the temple toward the east (for the temple faced east). The water was flowing down from below the south end of the threshold of the temple, south of the altar. Then he brought me out by way of the north gate and led me around on the outside to the outer gate that faces toward the east; and behold, the water was trickling out on the south side.

In representing the life-giving, nourishing Presence of God that the Holy Spirit administers, the water from the temple reaches the ends of the earth. The vision reveals that the temple is the source of God's Presence in the entire earth rather than in just one location. Once again, the new covenant temple is not a building but the people of God. This means that the people of God (i.e., the church) is how God's life-giving Presence and glory are to fill the creation (Rev. 22:1–5). Church Father Ambrose of Milan wrote:

The river flowing from the Throne of God is a figure of the Holy Spirit, but by the waters spoken of by David the powers of heaven are intended. The Kingdom of God is the work of the Spirit; and it is no matter for wonder if He reigns in this together with the Son, since St. Paul promises that we too shall reign with the Son.[3]

The Spirit Comforts the Church

The Holy Spirit comforts the church.[4] Acts 9:31 says: "So the church throughout all of Judea and Galilee and Samaria had peace and was being built up. And walking in fear of the Lord *and in the comfort of the Holy Spirit, it multiplied*" (italics added). In John 14:26, Jesus called the Holy Spirit the *parakaleitos,* variously translated "comforter" or "helper." The word means "the one who comes alongside of to encourage or strengthen." Jesus says in John 14:25–27:

> "These things I have spoken to you while I am still with you. But the Helper [*parakaleitos*], the Holy

---

3. Ambrose of Milan, "Three Books of St. Ambrose on the Holy Spirit" in *St. Ambrose: Select Works and Letters* (New York: Christian Literature Company, 1896), 156.

4. The translation "comfort" goes back to the King James Version in 1611. The word has Latin roots in *com fortis*. The sense is to strengthen or encourage. It does not have much of the affective overtones of modern English "comfort," with its sense of making an injured or grieving person feel better.

Spirit, whom the Father will send in my name, he will teach you all things and bring to your remembrance all that I have said to you. Peace I leave with you; my peace I give to you. Not as the world gives do I give to you. Let not your hearts be troubled, neither let them be afraid."

The context of this passage is that Jesus is preparing his disciples for his departure from them. He is easing any anxiety that could come with the idea that he will no longer be with them. He says that even though he will not be with them physically, he will be with them through the Holy Spirit. The Holy Spirit mediates the Presence of Jesus, which brings comfort. The Holy Spirit reminds Christians of Jesus's teaching to guide them in truth, and the trustworthiness of Jesus's teaching produces peace. By mediating the Presence of God in the church, the Holy Spirit's ministry is one of comfort and confidence in right teaching and guidance. The Holy Spirit carries on where Jesus left off in leading the way to a restored life in God.

> The Holy Spirit carries on where Jesus left off in leading the way to a restored life in God.

Relief from the Punishment for Sin

There is comfort that comes with relief from the shame and punishment for sin, "for to set the mind on the flesh is death, but to set the mind on the Spirit is life and peace" (Rom. 8:6). The replacement of sin-guilt with the righteousness of Christ is fresh, cold water on the parched tongue of the sinner, "for the wages of sin is death, but the free gift of God is eternal life in Christ Jesus our Lord" (Rom. 6:23). The burden of the righteousness of Christ is easy, and his yoke is light (Matt. 11:30) compared to the crushing weight of sin-guilt. Reconciliation with God brings peace (Rom. 5:1). For the heavy-laden sinner, Jesus made "peace through the blood of his cross" (Col. 1:20) and "there is therefore now no condemnation for those who are in Christ Jesus" (Rom. 8:1).

Rest from Wrestling with Inner Twistedness

There is also comfort with no longer wrestling with Adam's nature (the nature diseased by sin). Paul writes that Christ, "by abolishing in his flesh the enmity, which is the Law of commandments contained in ordinances, so that in Himself He might make the two into one new man, thus [established] peace" (Eph. 2:15 NASB). And that "the law of the Spirit of life has set you free in Christ Jesus from the law of sin and death" (Rom. 8:2). As the Holy Spirit empowers believers to overcome sin, he releases us from the constant battle with the sin condition. Temptation remains, but the crippling bent to sinning is corrected. Because of the empowering Presence of the Holy Spirit, the church need not be frustrated or exasperated over the guilt of a wavering, mediocre life in Christ. The Holy Spirit strengthens and firms up faith. He fortifies the church to be wholly committed to Jesus. He brings believers to the place where the sinful pining of the flesh continually diminishes in the blazing fire of a fully devoted heart. The divided heart is exhausted and frustrated. The guilt of having a divided heart is a constant draw on spiritual strength and energy. The Holy Spirit leads to the place of being able to firmly resist sin with an undivided, "perfect" heart.

> Temptation remains, but the crippling bent to sinning is corrected.

Help in Spiritual Warfare

The Holy Spirit also comforts the church militant during spiritual warfare while carrying out the Great Commission. Paul says in 2 Timothy 3:12: "Indeed, all who desire to live a godly life in Christ Jesus will be persecuted." Jesus says in John 15:18: "If the world hates you, know that it has hated me before it hated you."[5] Acts 9:31 (NRSVCE) tells us that the Holy Spirit comforted the early church even though they suffered much persecution. The text says: "Meanwhile, the church throughout Judea, Galilee, and Samaria had peace

---

5. See also John 15:19; Acts 14:22; 1 Peter 3:14; 4:12–14, 16; 1 John 3:13.

and was built up. Living in the fear of the Lord and in the comfort of the Holy Spirit, it increased in numbers."[6]

Witness, Holiness, and Unity

The work of the Holy Spirit to shape the church into the image of Christ (i.e., sanctification) makes Christ *visible* in the world. Enabling spiritual gifts (e.g., teaching, preaching, Christian service, faith, charity, fortitude, knowledge, piety, etc.), illuminating the Scriptures, animating worship, inspiring spiritual disciplines (e.g., prayer, fasting, study, solitude, etc.), comforting, healing, and protecting believers—*all* the ministries of the Holy Spirit—ultimately serve the greater goal of testifying to the lordship of Jesus.

When holiness is actualized in the church, faithful Christians put the image of God on display for the world to see. Holiness is a witness to the character of God through the people of God. Spirit-empowered obedience to the will of God sets believers apart from the world. When Christians are faithful, loving, kind, compassionate, hospitable, honest, gracious, and just, it testifies to the character of God to the world around them. As God is revealed in Jesus as the preeminent image-bearer, and believers conform to the image of Jesus through Holy Spirit indwelling, the world sees the witness of Jesus in the witness of the church.

---

6. See Matthew 5:10.

The most salient characteristic of the church's testimony is unity in love (John 13:35; 1 John 3:10). Christian unity is the ultimate witness to living in the fullness of the anointing of God as the people of God (Ps. 133). Believer unity is the sign of the image restored as it conforms to the self-giving character of the triune God. Holiness, when understood in these terms, is believer unity. At least in part, holiness is a church that is bound together in holy love. Christians are set apart from the world in that they love one another and their enemies. Other-oriented, self-giving love in the church is synonymous with conforming to the witness of Christ (Phil. 2:1–11). If Christ is the preeminent image of the triune God, and Christians partake in the very nature of God through Christ by the Holy Spirit, then there is a visible witness to the world of the nature of God. The Holy Spirit's goal to bring glory to Christ, then, is accomplished through the church's sanctification. In shaping the church to the image of Christ, Christ becomes visible and glorified.

> The most salient characteristic of the church's testimony is unity in love.

Gifts and Empowerment for Ministry

Spiritual gifts is one of the first things that comes to mind for Christians when they think of the Holy Spirit. This makes sense because of the story of Pentecost. When

Jesus pours out the Holy Spirit on the church in Acts 2, something *miraculous* happens: the apostles are given the gift of tongues to preach the gospel to their multilingual audience. The supernatural empowerment of gifts is a recurring theme in the rest of the book of Acts as well.

In the stories that follow Pentecost we read about the apostles healing people, casting out demons, being miraculously transported long distances, and many more. Essentially, the apostles are performing the same sorts of miracles that Jesus performed in his earthly ministry. What's happening here is that the ministry of Jesus and the proclamation of the kingdom come is continued in the apostles. The effect of this is not only that God frees individuals from various forms of the physical oppression of sin, but these miracles are testimonies to the fact that God is at work and doing something new. Just as Jesus's divine calling and commissioning was authenticated through his performing of miracles, so it is with the apostles. No one can deny that God has chosen these individuals for his purposes because of the supernatural testimony of gifts.

> Essentially, the apostles are performing the same sorts of miracles that Jesus performed in his earthly ministry.

The first instance of the Holy Spirit filling a person with the power for services is in Exodus 31. We read of Bezalel, whom the Holy Spirit empowered to build the tabernacle in this story. All Spirit empowerment is for the purpose of building the church. We also see the Holy Spirit empowering the judges as military heroes commissioned to deliver Israel from their slavery to foreign nations. Likewise, Saul and David are empowered to fulfill their roles as kings.[7] Throughout the Old Testament, the primary function of the Holy Spirit is to enable individuals to accomplish a God-given task or mission.

> Throughout the Old Testament, the primary function of the Holy Spirit is to enable individuals to accomplish a God-given task or mission.

Jesus is the most excellent example of Spirit-filled service. The dove's descent is both a public witness to Christ's unique relationship with the Father (Matt. 3:16) and the mark of empowerment for ministry (Luke 4:18–21). According to the Old Testament, one of the marks of the Messiah is that he is filled with the Holy Spirit to carry out his God-given mission (Isa. 11:2–3). Likewise, empowerment for ministry is the first order of business at Pentecost in Acts 2. Peter is empowered to preach once Jesus pours out the Holy Spirit on the disciples. In every instance that the Holy Spirit empowers a person for service, it is for the

---

7. See 1 Samuel 16:13. Cf. Moses in Numbers 11:26, Joshua in Deuteronomy 34:9, Ezekiel in 2:2, and Micah in 3:8.

sake of testimony—a witness to the real power of God in the world.

The Gifts of the Spirit

The gifts of the Spirit are discussed in three places in the Bible: Romans 12, 1 Corinthians 12, and Ephesians 4.[8] The gifts of the Spirit are:

- Apostleship (Eph. 4:11)
- Prophecy (1 Cor. 14:1)
- Evangelization (Eph. 4:11; Acts 21:8)
- Pastoring (Eph. 4:11)
- Teaching (Rom. 12:7)
- Confession (1 John 4:2)
- Exhortation (Rom. 12:8)
- Healing (1 Cor. 12:9, 28, 30)
- Miracles (1 Cor. 12:28)
- Ecstatic utterance (Acts 2:4, 8; 1 Cor. 12:10)
- Speaking in other languages (Acts 2:4, 8; 1 Cor. 12:10)
- Interpretation of other languages (Acts 2:4, 8; 1 Cor. 12:10)
- Discernment (1 Cor. 12:10)

---

8. See also 1 Peter 4:10.

- Serving (Rom. 12:7)
- Administration (1 Cor. 12:28)
- Faith (1 Cor. 12:9)
- Encouragement (Rom. 12:8)
- Ability to distinguish spirits (1 Cor. 12:10)
- Mercy and generosity (Rom. 12:8)
- Leadership, wisdom, and knowledge (Rom. 12:8; 1 Cor. 12:28)
- Love (1 Cor. 13)

Some scholars believe that when taken together, the various lists are exhaustive, while others take them to be representative. In any case, Paul repeatedly makes the point that the gifts are not for us but for others, which is consistent with the understanding previously expressed that to be God-like, to bear his image, is to be other-oriented. The person who is sanctified is empowered to use whatever gifts they have, whether great or small, for the good of others, without concern for themselves. This reality is fully expressed in the gift of love, which is the gift above all others and summarizes all others. Love is why gifts of the Spirit are always complementary to the whole. As Paul writes in 1 Corinthians 13:1–3:

> If I speak in the tongues of men and of angels, but have not love, I am a noisy gong or a clanging cymbal. And if I have prophetic powers, and understand all mysteries and all knowledge, and if I have

all faith, so as to remove mountains, but have not love, I am nothing. If I give away all I have, and if I deliver up my body to be burned, but have not love, I gain nothing.

As the text clearly says, the gifts are dispensed by the Spirit entirely as he wishes (1 Cor. 12:4, 11), with some people perhaps receiving several, and others receiving only one.

The Holy Spirit supernaturally empowers these abilities. Gifts are not merely a human talent developed over many years of hard work and focused practice and training. Our naturally born talents can be gifts of the Spirit, but we must surrender those gifts to the Spirit's control and use. If they have not been surrendered, they are deadly, steadily destroying us and not building up the church. They are unclean. When we surrender our gifts to the Spirit, we render them clean. They are no longer our own; they are his to employ for his saving work in the world.

It is also possible that God gives us an entirely new and unexpected gift in the moment of total surrender and entire sanctification. By the very nature of its giving, this gift will be clean. If we continue to surrender the gift to God, he can use it in ways unimaginable.

Cessationism vs. Continuationism

Some have argued that supernatural "sign gifts" ended with the apostles and are, therefore, not operative in the church after the first century. This view is known as "cessationism." Cessationism does not suggest that *all* spiritual gifts ceased with the apostles, but that the specific gifts that functioned as signs to authenticate that God was doing something new in salvation history have ceased. Those gifts usually include the gift of tongues, prophecy, miracles, healing, words of wisdom, and words of knowledge.

While a full treatment of this view is beyond the scope of this book, we can say here that there are two primary pieces of evidence to the view that sign gifts ended with the apostles. The first is that we simply don't encounter Holy Spirit–empowered miracles through gifts today like we read about in the books of Acts. The second support for cessationism is from 1 Corinthians 13:8, which says: "Love never ends. As for prophecies, *they will pass away*; as for tongues, *they will cease*; as for knowledge, *it will pass away*" (italics added).

Cessationism is in contrast with the continuationist view, which affirms that all gifts of the Spirit are still at

> Cessationism does not suggest that *all* spiritual gifts ceased with the apostles, but that the specific gifts that functioned as signs to authenticate that God was doing something new in salvation history have ceased.

work and active in the church today. I strongly affirm the continuationist view. While the biblical support and theological arguments for the continuationist view are long and many, I want to site just four here.⁹

First, the Bible nowhere distinguishes between "sign gifts" and other gifts in its explicit declarations, or in its overarching "subtext."¹⁰ The notion of sign gifts are imported into the text usually by those who affirm the cessationist view. In other words, this distinction is *foreign* to the Bible and, therefore, should be taken with caution.

Second, the Bible explicitly and definitively declares that the gifts of the Spirit are for the primary purpose of *building*

> The Bible explicitly and definitively declares that the gifts of the Spirit are for the primary purpose of building up the church.

---

9. For more information in the cessationist vs. continuationist debate, see Wayne Grudem, ed., *Are Miraculous Gifts for Today? Four Views* (Leicester: IVP, 1988); Jack Deere, *Surprised by the Power of the Spirit* (Eastbourne: Kingsway, 1994); John MacArthur, *Strange Fire: the Danger of Offending the Holy Spirit with Counterfeit Worship* (Nashville: Thomas Nelson, 2013); Michael L. Brown, *Authentic Fire: A Response to John MacArthur's Strange Fire* (Lake Mary, FL: Creation House, 2015).

10. The Bible does not contain the word *Trinity*, but the doctrine of the Trinity is certainly biblical when considering the whole council of the Word of God. Like the word *Trinity*, "sign gift" does not occur anywhere in the Bible. Unlike the word *Trinity*, however, the suggestion of such a classification is not suggested anywhere in the text.

up the church. This being the case, why would the operation of some of those gifts cease when the church never ceases needing to be built up, brought into maturity, and effective in fulfilling its mission in the world? It seems odd that God would take away some of the means by which the church is to be fully realized as the church is in its development while awaiting Christ's return.

Third, as Gregg Allison and Andreas Köstenberger state: "1 Corinthians 13:8–13 (also 1:7–8) places the cessation of spiritual gifts at the return of Christ, not before that event."[11] Again, cessationism argues that the sign gifts ceased with the apostles. What Paul is saying in this text, however, is that these gifts will cease *at the second coming of Christ*. This interpretation of 1 Corinthians 13:8–13 is resonant with the notion that gifts are for building up the church and the effective fulfillment of the church's mission on earth *until Christ's return.*

> "[Scripture] places the cessation of spiritual gifts at the return of Christ, not before that event."

Finally, history is on the side of continuationism. There are volumes of witness-affirmed testimonies in support of

---

11. Gregg R. Allison and Andreas J. Köstenberger, *The Holy Spirit*, Theology for the People of God, eds. David S. Dockery, Nathan A. Finn, and Christopher W. Morgan (Nashville: B&H Academic, 2020), 430.

the full operation of all of the gifts of the Spirit—even sign gifts—after the first century.[12]

While I strongly affirm the continuationist view for these (and other) reasons, I believe it is important to note that one's view on the matter does not rise to the level of dogma. That is, it does not impact one's salvation. That the Holy Spirit is the third person of the Trinity who is fully God and eternally proceeds from the Father through the Son and is coequal, coeternal, and indivisibly united with God the Father and the Son *is essential for Christian orthodoxy.* All Christians everywhere and always have confessed such. Any teaching that deviates from that confession is a departure from the historical, orthodox, and apostolic faith. One's view on which gifts are operative in the church today are not in the same category as the doctrine of the divine personhood of the Holy Spirit. That is, cessationists and continuationists can worship together as brothers and sisters in Christ while maintaining their theological differences.

> God chooses to accomplish his redemptive purposes *through* his human agents.

Even with the differences between cessationism and continuationism, there is agreement that at least some of the gifts of the Spirit are operative today for the sake of

---

12. See Craig Keener's *Miracles Today: The Supernatural Work of God in the Modern World* (Grand Rapids: Baker Academic, 2021).

building up the church and supernaturally enabling the church to fulfill the Great Commission. Furthermore, there is agreement that God chooses to accomplish his redemptive purposes *through his human agents*. This is evident through the simple fact that God commands us to *pray*. There are certain things that God accomplishes in the world on his own apart from human agency. There are other things, however, that God wishes to accomplish for which he invites our participation. The Holy Spirit *prompts* his people to pray for God to work, to intervene, to comfort, to convict, and ultimately to redeem.

Gifts and Power over Sin

Ultimately, the great miracle of the Christian faith is that God has enjoined himself to human flesh in Jesus Christ and, therefore, brings us into holy fellowship with himself through the Holy Spirit. This results in the new creation of a new kind of human. It means the full restoration of the image of God as it was always intended and perfectly revealed in Jesus Christ. Jesus, as the image of God and example of what humanity was always supposed to be, did things outside of the realm of possibility for members of Adam's race. This means that the witness of Christ's miracles does not merely point to that fact that the kingdom has come. *The witness of Christ's miracles also points to what the image restored looks like.* Andrew Louth writes:

To be human is to be in the image, and being in the image, according to the image, entails a relationship to Christ, who is the image. Certainly he is an image in virtue of being the Word of God, the *Logos*, God's self-manifestation; but this is something we only fully understand through the Incarnation. Human kind is created according to an image—the Word of God—that we only truly know through the Incarnation. It is only through the Incarnation that we can truly understand what it is to be human.... And the Fall only reinforces this. What we know from our experience of being human is what it is to be fallen humanity, but to be in the image is, at the very least, to bear some trace of true humanity, unfallen humanity, and it is unfallen humanity that we see in Christ. For the Word of God, in becoming man, became what we were meant to be. To be human is to have a nature with capacities, faculties, that are never properly realized in our fallen state; we have a glimpse of these faculties in Christ.[13]

> When we cooperate with God's divine grace, we become fully human by the indwelling of the Holy Spirit.

---

13. Andrew Louth, *Introducing Eastern Orthodox Theology* (London: SPCK, 2013), 87.

On this basis, Louth goes on to write that "it is a mistake to see the miracles as simply evidence of Christ's divinity.... *They are evidence of the potentialities of the human, cooperating with divine grace.*"[14]

When we cooperate with God's divine grace, we become fully human by the indwelling of the Holy Spirit. Normally we think about freedom from the power of sin *within*. The freedom from sin goes beyond this, however. When we become fully human, supernatural things happen that lift us—and those around us—out of the mire of a world defined, but not determined, by the sin condition. Gifts, then, are an external extension of victory over the power of sin made possible only by the Holy Spirit. Gifts are signs that the kingdom of God is breaking into the present reality; that Christ has been victorious over sin both within and without.

Conclusion

The Holy Spirit is at work in the salvation of individuals and the collective body of Christ. As Christians, the Holy Spirit unites us with one another in Christ and joins us with the life of the holy Trinity. Union with Christ is what constitutes the church. The Holy Spirit works for believers and in believers and works through the collective body of Christ to

---

14. Louth, 88, italics added.

advance the kingdom of God. Ultimately, salvation is about the restoration of the Presence of God with his people. Jesus makes that possible, and the Holy Spirit carries it out through personal indwelling. There is fruit that comes from that indwelling that builds toward the final consummation of the triune God's redemptive purposes.

Why It Matters

We said in previous sections that salvation is about what God does for us, in us, and through us. The Holy Spirit not only transforms us, but he also transforms the world through us. The work of the Spirit also enables us to be agents of transformation in other people's lives. He sets us free to work alongside him in liberating the captives. He bestows gifts and graces to bring life and light to a dying and dark world. God chose that his salvation would come to the world through a people. This means us, the body of Christ. Without the church's holiness and the redeeming activity and ministry of the saints in a diseased world, no one will see the Lord. When thinking about what it means to be saved or a Christian, we must remember that mission is an integral part of the big picture. Christianity is not a spectator sport. It's not about simply another way to self-help or the actualization of our true selves. It's about the other-oriented nature of the image of God restored. As Paul puts it, it's about having the same mind that is in Christ, doing nothing out of selfish ambition or conceit, but in humility, counting others more significant than ourselves. It means looking not to our interests but the interest of others (Phil. 2:2–4).

Questions for Reflection

1. What is the church?
2. What does subsisting relations have to do with the church, Christ, and the Holy Spirit?
3. How are gifts of the Spirit different than human talents?
4. In what ways does the Holy Spirit comfort the church?

CHAPTER 8

The Holy Spirit and End Times

The resurrection of Jesus launched the new age of the Spirit, which was consummated at Pentecost. James Dunn comments on Pentecost:

> For once again we stand at a watershed in salvation-history, the beginning of the new age and the new covenant, not for Jesus this time, but now for his disciples. What Jordan was to Jesus, Pentecost was to his disciples. As Jesus entered the new age and covenant by being baptized in the Spirit at Jordan, so the disciples followed him in like manner at Pentecost. With the wider enjoyment of the messianic age made possible by Jesus' representative death, so at Pentecost the new covenant, hitherto confined to the one representative man, was extended to embrace all those who

remained faithful to him and tarried at Jerusalem in obedience to his command.[1]

The outpouring of the Holy Spirit at Pentecost consummated that new age. Pentecost, then, is the beginning of the end. The giving of the Holy Spirit inaugurates the long-awaited new creation. Ultimately, God promised to redeem not only Israel and the rest of humanity from death and corruption, but God also promised to redeem the entire creation (Gen. 3:15; 12:1–4; 18:18; 22:18). He promised to save everything that was lost.

> The giving of the Holy Spirit inaugurates the long-awaited new creation.

Much in the same way that the Holy Spirit was an active part in the events of the first creation (Gen. 1:1), he will play a crucial role once again in birthing the new creation.[2]

The Resurrection and the New Era

The connection between the Holy Spirit and the end comes through the resurrection of Jesus as the single most

---

[1]. James Dunn, *Baptism in the Holy Spirit* (Philadelphia: Westminster, 1970), 40.

[2]. Also note that Mary was "found to be with child from the Holy Spirit" (Matt. 1:18). Even in the creative event of the incarnation of Jesus, the Holy Spirit was central.

important event in history. The resurrection of Jesus sets history on a different trajectory. Everything that we know about human life is turned on its head when Jesus walks out of the grave and ascends into heaven (Rom. 5:19). Death, the master of all and the one thing that cannot be defeated by human innovation, Jesus overcomes. Jesus's resurrection means that death is no longer the single reference point for all created life. It is by the Holy Spirit that he was raised. The Holy Spirit brought light to darkness and order to chaos in Genesis, and he does it again by raising Jesus (Rom. 1:2). Thanks to Jesus and the Holy Spirit, Christians live in a new age—an age that God promised would come.

After the resurrection of Christ, the Holy Spirit continues to bring the old age of the flesh to a close through his work in and through the church. In particular, the Holy Spirit empowers the church to witness to the new creation that God has inaugurated through the resurrection and glorification of Jesus. The Holy Spirit's role in sanctifying believers is a testimony that the new age of the Spirit has arrived. Christians are walking, breathing evidence that a new era has come. The work of the Holy Spirit functions to testify to the new age in such a way that the world would look upon the church and be drawn to it as something

> The work of the Holy Spirit functions to testify to the new age in such a way that the world would look upon the church and be drawn to it as something genuinely new.

genuinely new. There is to be freedom among believers that is visible to the world. As the Holy Spirit sanctifies the church, the church's testimony is strengthened, and the new creation multiplies. More and more individuals are baptized into the family of faith and born into the new creation. As the church grows, so does the dominion of Christ. As the dominion of Christ advances, the end comes rushing forward into the present.

The Holy Spirit also cooperates with the other two members of the Trinity to bring about the new creation through the church. In a sense, the Spirit is the breath of God that carries the Word (Jesus) that brings life and light into death and darkness. G. K. Beale writes:

> Just as God's breathing into Adam made him alive and a part of the first creation, so Jesus's breathing into the disciples the Spirit might well be considered an act incorporating them into a stage of new creation, which Jesus had inaugurated already by his resurrection. As such beings of the new age, they are to announce the life-giving forgiveness that can come only from Christ (John 20:23), the center and the foundation of the new creation. Here again, therefore, we see the Spirit as the transformer of people into the life of the new creation.[3]

---

3. G. K. Beale, *A New Testament Biblical Theology: The Unfolding of the Old Testament in the New* (Grand Rapids: Baker Academic, 2011), 572.

Pentecost is not merely the day that God gives the Spirit to the church; it is the day when the new creation through resurrection becomes realized; the day when the victory over death becomes available to all the world. This era of the new creation is what Paul calls "the new age of the Spirit." It is a time in which Spirit-filled believers no longer live under the tyranny of sin, but rather, live according to the Spirit in perfect obedience to Christ as King.

The Kingdom Is Now and Not Yet

While God launched the new era of the new creation in the resurrection of Jesus and the giving of the Holy Spirit, the old age of sin and death is temporarily present in the world. The resurrection of Jesus is the beginning of the end. Jesus came once to launch the new age of the Spirit, and he will come again to put an end to the old age of the flesh. Everett Ferguson writes:

> Through Christ the End, or the beginning of the End, has come. Tomorrow is here today. Something of God's glory and power has reached down and called people for the coming age. The kingdom of God has created a new people, the church. But all this is only a down payment. Much more awaits the final consummation of God's purposes. Nevertheless, the imagery of first fruits and first installment indicates the life in the world to come and its blessings

will be in continuity with the present. Those who share the kingdom now will be those to participate in it in the future.[4]

The kingdom of God, then, is both now, but also not yet. Now, believers experience freedom from the power of sin through the indwelling of the Holy Spirit. Believers experience a spiritual rebirth in the present. At the same time, believers anticipate a future physical rebirth in the resurrection to come (1 Cor. 15:51–57; 1 Thess. 4:16–17). The Holy Spirit is the agent through whom spiritual and physical rebirth occurs (Rom. 8:12–14).

> Defeatism interprets Romans 7 as the normal Christian life. However, the Bible teaches that those in Christ can be free from the power of sin and sinning.

That the kingdom is both now and not yet means that Christians live in a tension between defeatism and triumphalism. Defeatism emphasizes the reality that salvation is not yet complete while we await the second coming and the consummation of the kingdom of heaven in the return of Jesus. Defeatism loves the phrase, "Well, I am and will always be a sinner," which undermines the power, the promise, and the Presence of the Holy Spirit as well as the efficacy of Christ's work. Defeatism interprets Romans 7 as the

---

4. Everett Ferguson, *The Church of Christ: A Biblical Ecclesiology for Today* (Grand Rapids: Eerdmans, 1996), 35.

normal Christian life. However, the Bible teaches that those in Christ can be free from the power of sin and sinning (Rom. 6) because of the fullness of the Holy Spirit.

On the other hand, it is likewise a mistake to believe that since the kingdom is now, we ought to be able to have enough faith to overcome infirmities, poverty, and ultimately death in this era. Stories of God performing miraculous healings (starting with the stories in the New Testament) are present indicators of future hope. At the same time, there are other stories of when God did not heal people miraculously in ways anticipated. This is because the kingdom, while now, is also not yet. Corruption, death, and decay reign over the physical creation until Christ's second coming and the consummation of the kingdom.

The Holy Spirit as the Seal

This present and future dynamic of the Holy Spirit is communicated in the metaphor of the Holy Spirit as *seal* (2 Cor. 1:21–22; Eph. 1:13; 4:30).[5] The Holy Spirit as seal emphasizes that the Holy Spirit is a present mark of a future reality yet to be fulfilled. This is also conceptualized as a down payment on a later inheritance. Gordon Fee writes:

> The Spirit is the evidence that the *eschatological promises of Paul's Jewish heritage have been fulfilled.*

---

5. See also Romans 5:5 and 8:9.

At the same time, the Spirit as God's empowering presence enables the people of God not simply to endure the present as they await the final consummation, but to do so with verve (with "spirit" if you will). And that is because the future is as sure as the presence of the Spirit as an experienced reality, hence the significance of the dynamic and experiential nature of the Spirit's coming into the life of the believer.[6]

The Holy Spirit as seal is an indicator of those who will be saved in the final judgment. Those who live a life free from the condemnation of sin are those who conform to the image of Christ and will be with him upon his return. While Christians live a life free from sin in the present, the evil powers of the world still condemn Christians as guilty, as they did Christ. The final condemnation of sin-guilt is death. The resurrection of the body, then, is the final vindication of Christ and his body of believers as those who have escaped the wages of sin. Just as the Holy Spirit empowers a life free from sin now, he is also the one who enacts the

> Just as the Holy Spirit empowers a life free from sin now, he is also the one who enacts the bodily resurrection in the future.

---

6. Gordon D. Fee, *God's Empowering Presence: The Holy Spirit in the Letters of Paul* (Grand Rapids: Baker Academic, 2011), 808.

bodily resurrection in the future. Christ was first vindicated as the Son of God through his resurrection by the Holy Spirit (Rom. 1:2; 1 Tim. 3:16). He is the first fruit of the resurrection (1 Cor. 15:23)—the representative head of the new creation that is the church. Likewise, those in Christ by the Holy Spirit will also be vindicated and declared victorious in the final judgment.

Conclusion

Pentecost marked the beginning of the end. When Jesus poured out the Holy Spirit on his followers, he launched the new age of the Spirit in which Christians can live free from the guilt and power of sin. Sanctified believers are the mark of those who will be saved from the final judgment. The mark of the faithful Christian whom God will vindicate in the last days is the fullness of the Spirit. That vindication is resurrection in the Holy Spirit.

Why It Matters

It is important as Christians that we know who we are, where we are from, and what time it is. The Christian worldview believes that history is going somewhere. Most non-Christian worldviews believe that history is simply on repeat; that all events that occur are simply a recurring cycle. The Bible refutes this. The Bible reveals that history is linear, not cyclical, and that God is working out his plan in time and space to redeem his creation. This means that there will be an end to sin, corruption, decay, suffering, and ultimately death. Knowing that there is an end coming informs the way that we live today. As Christians, we live today as if Jesus could return at any moment, and that upon his return we will be vindicated as faithful in God's eyes.

Questions for Reflection

1. What does the resurrection have to do with the end times?
2. What do we mean when we say the kingdom is both now, but also not yet?
3. In what way is the Holy Spirit a seal regarding the return of Jesus?
4. What is the age of the Spirit?

CHAPTER 9

The Holy Spirit and the Holy Life

We began our journey with Moses and the burning bush. In that story, God commanded Moses to take off his sandals because he was standing on holy ground. The ground was holy because God's personal, holy Presence was in the bush. This whole encounter happened in the desert at the foot of Mount Sinai.

Interestingly, this story takes place in *the desert*. In the Bible, the desert is an *unholy* place. It's lifeless and harsh. It's where demons dwell. Satan tempted Jesus in the desert because the desert is the seat of government for the powers of darkness. The desert is the place of the curse. It is the place of death. The absence of life in the desert results from the absence of God, the Giver of Life. Once again, the desert is, above all other places, *unholy*.

Victor Hamilton points out that "God has a way of showing up at unexpected places such as bushes."[1] He says:

> It was at a bush that he appeared to Hagar ... and it was at a bush that he first appeared to Moses. And speaking of God showing up at unexpected places, perhaps one might see a parallel between the angel of the Lord appearing in the middle of nowhere to a shepherding Moses to make an important announcement and the angels showing up to a group of shepherds in the middle of nowhere to make an important announcement (Luke 2:8–20).[2]

Another one of those unexpected places that God shows up in fiery fashion is at Pentecost when the Holy Spirit descended on a group of fishermen and tax collectors. Soon after that, he even descended on Gentiles (Acts 10). In the broader context of the biblical story, fishermen, tax collectors, and Gentiles were "unholy ground." Of all the holy people and holy places in the world, these were the least of them. These were the outsiders, not the temple priests and scribes. These were the equivalent of unholy desert ground.

It must have been a shock to Moses to hear God say that this desert ground surrounding this bush was *holy*.

---

1. Victor P. Hamilton, *Handbook on the Pentateuch*, 2nd ed. (Grand Rapids: Baker Academic, 2005), 141.
2. Hamilton, 141.

In Moses's mind, that's impossible. Places like Egypt and Canaan were holy places, not the desert. The gods dwell in lush gardens with perfect climates and plenty of food and drink, not in places like this, not in the place of curse and outcast. In this moment of coming to grips with the notion that God's Presence can make this cursed ground holy, perhaps Moses wondered: *If God can make this ground holy, can he make me holy?*

The desert is a lot like the human heart. It is the place of the curse, profane and utterly unholy. It is home to the powers of evil. It is absence of God's blessing and life-giving Presence. In the story of the burning bush, God's holy Presence fills the heart of the bush yet doesn't consume it. His Presence is so pure, so incorruptibly good, and so powerfully life-giving that it entirely sanctifies the place of its dwelling. This is the story of the divine Presence *via* the Holy Spirit coming home to the human heart. Because of Jesus, the Holy Spirit can rush into our hearts yet not destroy us. He can reverse the curse. He can make the place of the curse a holy habitation that is blessed with life and the fruit of life.

> The desert is a lot like the human heart. It is the place of the curse, profane and utterly unholy.

My point has two prongs. First, Jesus came for the sick, not for the healthy. Mark 2:15–17 says:

> And as he reclined at table in his house, many tax collectors and sinners were reclining with Jesus

and his disciples, for there were many who followed him. And the scribes of the Pharisees, when they saw that he was eating with sinners and tax collectors, said to his disciples, "Why does he eat with tax collectors and sinners?" And when Jesus heard it, he said to them, "Those who are well have no need of a physician, but those who are sick. I came not to call the righteous, but sinners."

In other words, the proclamation of the gospel—the message of freedom from the guilt and power of sin—is for those who know they need it (Matt. 5:3). It is for hearts the Holy Spirit has softened.

> His Presence breaks into the darkest places of our lives and turns deserts to gardens.

Second—and directly related to the first—no ground is too unholy for God's Presence to take up residence. His Presence breaks into the darkest places of our lives and turns deserts to gardens.

Graveyards to Gardens

In the story of the resurrection, Jesus turned a graveyard into a garden. Graveyards, like deserts, are unholy places. They are the place of death. In the Gospels, we find the demoniac in the graveyard (Mark 5:1–20). Cemeteries are home to the powers of darkness because they reign over the kingdom of death. When Jesus goes into a graveyard—and a grave in the case of the resurrection—exciting things happen. After three days in the tomb, Jesus came back to life.

The first detail of the story that we encounter in the resurrection story according to John is: "Now on the first day of the week [new creation language] Mary Magdalene came to the tomb early, while it was still dark, and saw that the stone had been taken away from the tomb" (John 20:1). Then, with tears in her eyes and the dawn breaking into the darkness of night, Mary sees the resurrected Lord and mistakes him for the *gardener*. This is one of my favorite moments in Scripture. I love this moment because the gardener is *exactly* who Jesus is. Jesus is the true gardener. Jesus is the Adam as he was always meant to be. Jesus, now with a resurrected body, is ready to launch the new age of the Spirit into the new creation. In this moment, Jesus makes the unholy ground of a graveyard into the garden of the new creation.

> Even though we have set our faces against God, Jesus's perfect sacrifice *worked*.

What's the significance of this? No ground is too unholy for Jesus to redeem. He turns desert ground into holy ground, and he turns a graveyard into the launchpad for the new creation. Every human heart is totally depraved. Every one of us has a diabolical, self-consuming inward bent. Even though we have set our faces against God, Jesus's perfect sacrifice *worked*. The full obedience and righteousness of

Christ was enough to remove every barrier between God and us. The blood of Jesus is powerful enough to purify every fiber of the human heart. This means that the Holy Spirit, based on the work of Christ, can fill us *in every part*. God likes showing up in unexpected places, even those places of our hearts that we may think unredeemable.

The holy life is available to all. Because of the redeeming work of the eternal, all-powerful, transcendent Holy Trinity, we can be free from the guilt and power of sin, and be completely filled with the perfect, holy love of God. The work of Christ at Calvary for us is sufficient to make perfect peace between God and us. The work of the Holy Spirit is enough to bring the perfect, holy love of God rushing into our hearts, and his ability to heal our diseased nature makes us useful instruments in his hands to participate in his mission to redeem the world.

The Means of Grace: God's Way In

But where does the rubber meet the road for lasting inner transformation? We have demonstrated that the Holy Spirit can soften our hearts, regenerate us, and uproot sin in our lives, but *how* does that happen practically? How does spiritual renewal and formation happen? Many people want to believe that there is a silver bullet answer to this question. We want to think that a one-off filling of the Holy Spirit is all we need and we're good to go.

On the one hand, Jesus teaches that if we want the Holy Spirit, all we need to do is ask. He says, "If you then, who are evil, know how to give good gifts to your children, how much more will the heavenly Father give the Holy Spirit to those who ask him!" (Luke 11:13). Add to this the instantaneous, dramatic transformation and empowerment of the disciples on the day of Pentecost. As we have laid out in detail in chapter 6, the regenerating work of the Holy Spirit and initial sanctification takes place in an instant. Yet, in gradual and entire sanctification, the Holy Spirit's ongoing work of attacking the root of sin is a process that requires our grace-enabled cooperation. What does our cooperation look like? How do we actually get into God's Presence? Better yet, how do we get God's Presence into us?

The answer is the *means of grace*. The means of grace are God-ordained activities and spiritual disciplines through which God gives grace. As John Wesley put it: "By 'means of grace' I understand outward signs, words, or actions ordained by God, and appointed for this end—to be the ordinary channels whereby he might convey to men preventing, justifying, and sanctifying grace."[3] We firmly established

> The means of grace are God-ordained activities and spiritual disciplines through which God gives grace.

---

3. John Wesley, Sermon 12 "The Means of Grace," https://www.umcdiscipleship.org/resources/john-wesley-on-the-means-of-grace.

that it is the Presence of God *via* the Holy Spirit that transforms us. The means of grace are ordained ways to enter his Presence. Jesus said, "For where two or three are gathered in my name, there am I among them" (Matt. 18:20). In other words, Jesus promises to meet us when we pray together. The psalmist also says that God's Presence is ushered into our midst when we worship him (Ps. 22:3). Prayer and worship are two ways of opening the door of our heart to the Holy Spirit.

John Wesley divided means of grace into two categories: (1) works of piety and (2) works of mercy. Let's explore each of these.

Works of Piety

Works of piety are interior works. They are often synonymous with the inward spiritual disciplines for seeking God. Works of piety are things like prayer (Matt. 6:5–15), fasting (Matt. 6:16), worship (Ps. 22:3), Bible study (Pss. 1, 19, and 119), taking Communion (Luke 22:19), Christian fellowship (Heb. 10:25), meditation (Ps. 1), and confession (James 5:16). When we do these things, we draw close to God. We quiet ourselves to hear the guidance of the Holy Spirit in leading us in the process of dying to self. In the quietness of our hearts, he illuminates our sin and empowers us to overcome that sin. In Deuteronomy, Moses commands that God's people practice the means of grace. He says:

"Hear, O Israel: The LORD our God, the LORD is one. You shall love the LORD your God with all your heart and with all your soul and with all your might. And these words that I command you today shall be on your heart. You shall teach them diligently to your children, and shall talk of them when you sit in your house, and when you walk by the way, and when you lie down, and when you rise. You shall bind them as a sign on your hand, and they shall be as frontlets between your eyes. You shall write them on the doorposts of your house and on your gates." (Deut. 6:4–9)[4]

In a similar vein, the psalmist says that the man who is blessed by the Presence of God delights in the word of God and meditates on it day and night (Ps. 1:2). He writes: "He is like a tree planted by streams of water that yields its fruit in its season, and its leaf does not wither. In all that he does, he prospers. The wicked are not so, but are like chaff that the wind drives away" (Ps. 1:3–4).

> The one who practices works of piety is *spiritually healthy.*

In other words, the one who practices works of piety is *spiritually healthy*. A tree that bears fruit in its season and whose leaf does not wither is healthy. It is a

---

4. See also Joshua 1:7–8.

tree that has all the nutrients it needs to thrive. The Holy Spirit provides these nutrients through the works of piety.

Works of Mercy

Works of mercy are external works of service unto others. This includes activities like serving the needs of the poor and visiting the sick and imprisoned. The best way to become selfless is by practicing selflessness. Obeying Christ's command to go into the world and to serve the needy is a means for sanctification in our lives. We don't usually think of service to others as therapeutic. Normally we think of service to others as tiring, frustrating, and complicated. However, when we serve the poor out of a place of total submission to God and by the empowerment of the Holy Spirit, we find that it is a healing balm to our souls. Works of mercy are therapeutic for one reason: when we serve others, the Holy Spirit fills us up. God's healing Presence is restored to us when we obey him.

Conclusion

While our sanctification is the work of the Holy Spirit enabled by grace, the commands of Scripture to practice the means of grace make it clear that our participation is necessary. The holy life is not simply a one-and-done deal that is complete with the baptism of the Holy Spirit. Baptism of the Holy Spirit launches us into a life of hunger and devotion for God, as well as holy desires. The Holy Spirit empowers us to obey Jesus's command to love our neighbors through action. Being filled with love leads to works driven by love and compassion. The Holy Spirit gives us a hunger for more of the divine Presence. The means of grace are places where the Holy Spirit satisfies that hunger to get the life of God deeper into us.

> Baptism of the Holy Spirit launches us into a life of hunger and devotion for God, as well as holy desires.

Why It Matters

God desires our sanctification. Paul says, "For this is the will of God, *your sanctification*: that you abstain from sexual immorality; that each one of you know how to control his own body in holiness and honor, not in the passion of lust like the Gentiles who do not know God" (1 Thess. 4:3–5, italics added). As Christians, the Holy Spirit reorders our desires to match the desires of God. We must walk in step with God's desires above our own. This means practicing holiness.

Furthermore, without the sanctification of the church, the world will not see Jesus. One of the central purposes of holiness is *mission*. Failing to actively pursue holiness through the means of grace will weaken our testimony to the reality that God can, in fact, transform people.

Questions for Reflection

1. What are the means of grace?
2. Which of the means of grace are hardest for you to practice?
3. How often do you practice the means of grace?
4. Practicing the means of grace should be a natural desire. Why?

CONCLUSION

The role of the Holy Spirit in the life of the Christian is indispensable. Without the Holy Spirit the church has no breath, no life, no vitality. Without the Holy Spirit, the kingdom of God remains unseen and distant. Without the Holy Spirit heaven and earth cannot be joined together and God cannot dwell in and among us. Without the Holy Spirit Jesus is inaccessible to a world in desperate need of a savior. Most important, without the Holy Spirit, God's aim to inhabit and reign over the creation alongside of his image-bearers is thwarted.

With the Holy Spirit, however, Jesus takes up residence in a broken world. By means of the Holy Spirit Jesus is embodied in time and space. He tabernacles among us (John 1:14). With the Holy Spirit the light of heaven chases away the darkness and tyranny of a broken and corrupt world. With the Holy Spirit the kingdom of God becomes not only visible, but also inhabitable, tangible, and real.

All this happens *through the church*. The Holy Spirit makes the kingdom of God visible and the Presence of Christ incarnate in the world precisely because he abides in believers.

This is a high calling. It is nothing short of a call to holiness for the redemption of the world.

The fulfillment of Christ's promise of the perennially abiding Presence of the Holy Spirit with the church (both collectively and with individual believers) is the basis of the Christian testimony. As the Holy Spirit imprints the holy, loving, and self-giving character of Christ on the hearts of believers, he activates and animates the church's testimony to the powerful and very real and righteous reign of Christ in the world. The Holy Spirit is essential for the fulfillment of God's plan to redeem the world through the church, the body of Christ. The church is called to be a kingdom of priests—mediators of reconciliation between God and the world.

Considering humanity's capacity for evil, this calling seems out of reach, a task too tall. The hope of the world, however, is not *merely* human. The hope of the world is *Christ in humanity* (Col. 1:27). It is through the repentant, the humble, the meek, the merciful, the peacemakers, the pure of heart, and those who seek righteousness that the Holy Spirit glorifies Jesus in the world. Therefore, the narrow way to the kingdom is through the desert. It is through John the Baptist's ministry of repentance that the way is prepared for Jesus and his kingdom to come.

But conviction—the recognition of wrong and the overwhelming sense of regret and remorse for wrongdoing—runs against the grain of the rock-hard, proud, and rebellious heart of humanity. Humans are depraved and desperately need help. More than anything else, we need help humbling ourselves. It is painful, terrifying, and takes no small amount of courage. It takes a miracle. It takes grace. It takes a Helper.

> Knowing that Jesus sends a Helper is a reminder that the world need not be dismayed, discouraged, defeated, nor stranded in sin.

The command that Jesus gives Christians to be perfect (Matt. 5:48) does not attest to humanity's potential for becoming trophies for God's trophy room; rather, it attests to the incomprehensible power of the Holy Spirit to humble the proud and redeem the broken. Once again, the Holy Spirit is our Helper.

Knowing that Jesus sends a Helper is a reminder that the world need not be dismayed, discouraged, defeated, nor stranded in sin. Greater is the Holy Spirit who is in believers than he who is in the world (1 John 4:4). Where he is, there is freedom (2 Cor. 3:17). And this isn't some esoteric freedom, this is a very real freedom that we can see, feel, and touch.

This is a freedom from sin and sinning. This is a freedom to live as God intended humans to live. It is nothing short of new birth.

This is a real freedom that translates into Christian maturity, which means overcoming temptation *regularly* (1 Cor. 10:13) to establish a new pattern of obedience and conformity to the life that the New Testament describes, and Jesus promises here and now (Rom. 7:25a). Not just obedience in our members, but obedience in our attitudes, and even our thoughts as far as they go deep down into the unreachable subterranean human subconscious. This freedom is *complete* because we have help, and that Helper is the powerful third person of the holy Trinity who is full of grace and truth. The Helper is God himself. He shares in the divine nature and possesses the sovereignty and wisdom of both the Father and Son. Through the Holy Spirit, the Presence of Jesus—the true Image-Bearer and victor over sin and death—is with us *always*.

BIBLIOGRAPHY

Allison, Gregg. "Eternal Processions" in *The Baker Compact Dictionary of Theological Terms*. Grand Rapids: Baker Books, 2016.

Allison, Gregg and Andreas J. Köstenberger. *The Holy Spirit*. Theology for the People of God. Edited by David S. Dockery, Nathan A. Finn, and Christopher W. Morgan. Nashville: B&H Academic, 2020.

Ambrose of Milan, "Three Books of St. Ambrose on the Holy Spirit," in *St. Ambrose: Select Works and Letters*, ed. Philip Schaff and Henry Wace, trans. H. de Romestin, E. de Romestin, and H. T. F. Duckworth, vol. 10 of *A Select Library of the Nicene and Post-Nicene Fathers of the Christian Church*. Second Series. New York: Christian Literature Company, 1896.

———. "Two Books Concerning Repentance" in *St. Ambrose: Select Works and Letters*. Edited by Philip Schaff and Henry Wace. Translated by H. de Romestin, E. de Romestin, and H. T. F. Duckworth. Volume 10 of *A Select Library of the Nicene and Post-Nicene Fathers of the Christian Church*. Second Series. New York: Christian Literature Company, 1896.

Athanasius of Alexandria. "On the Incarnation of the Word," in *St. Athanasius: Select Works and Letters*. Edited by Philip Schaff and Henry Wace. Translated by Archibald T. Robertson. Volume 4 of *A Select Library of the Nicene and Post-Nicene Fathers of the Christian Church*. Second Series. New York: Christian Literature Company, 1892.

Barclay, John M. G. *Paul and the Gift*. Grand Rapids; Cambridge, U.K.: William B. Eerdmans Publishing Company, 2015.

Barth, Karl. *Church Dogmatics IV/2: The Doctrine of Reconciliation*. London: T&T Clark, 1958.

Basil of Caesarea. "The Book of Saint Basil on the Spirit," in *St. Basil: Letters and Select Works*. Edited by Philip Schaff and Henry Wace. Translated by Blomfield Jackson. Volume 8 of *A Select Library of the Nicene and Post-Nicene Fathers of the Christian Church*. Second Series. New York: Christian Literature Company, 1895.

Beale, G. K. *A New Testament Biblical Theology: The Unfolding of the Old Testament in the New*. Grand Rapids: Baker Academic, 2011.

Bird, Michal F. and Scott Harrower, eds. *Trinity without Hierarchy: Reclaiming Nicene Orthodoxy in Evangelical Theology*. Grand Rapids: Kregal, 2019.

Block, Daniel I. *The Book of Ezekiel: Chapters 25–48*. The New International Commentary on the Old Testament. Grand Rapids: Eerdmans, 1998.

Burke, Trevor J. and Keith Warrington, eds. *A Biblical Theology of the Holy Spirit*. London: SPCK, 2014.

Cairnes, Alan. *Dictionary of Theological Terms: A Ready Reference of Over 800 Theological and Doctrinal Terms*. Greenville, SC: Ambassador Emerald International, 2002.

Catholic Church. *Catechism of the Catholic Church*, 2nd ed. Washington, DC: United States Catholic Conference, 2000.

Cole, Graham A. *He Who Gives Life: The Doctrine of the Holy Spirit*. Foundations of Evangelical Theology. Edited by John S. Feinberg. Wheaton, IL: Crossway Books, 2007.

Collins, Kenneth J. *The Theology of John Wesley: Holy Love and the Shape of Grace*. Nashville: Abingdon Press, 2007.

Collins, Kenneth J. and Jason E. Vickers. *The Sermons of John Wesley: A Collection for the Christian Journey*. Nashville: Abingdon Press, 2013.

Crisp, Oliver D. and Fred Sanders, eds. *The Third Person of the Trinity: Explorations in Constructive Dogmatics*. Grand Rapids: Zondervan, 2020.

Deasley, Alex R. G. "Entire Sanctification and the Baptism with the Holy Spirit: Perspectives on the Biblical View of the Relationship." Volume 14.1, Spring 1979 in the *Wesleyan Theological Journal*, 27–44.

Dunn, James. *Baptism in the Holy Spirit*. Philadelphia: Westminster, 1970.

———. *Baptism in the Holy Spirit: A Re-Examination of the New Testament Teaching on the Gift of the Spirit in Relation to Pentecostalism Today.* 2nd ed. London: SCM Press, 2010.

Fee, Gordon D. *God's Empowering Presence: The Holy Spirit in the Letters of Paul.* Grand Rapids: Baker Academic, 2011.

Ferguson, Everett. *The Church of Christ: A Biblical Ecclesiology for Today.* Grand Rapids: Eerdmans, 1996.

Ferguson, Sinclair B. *The Holy Spirit.* Edited by Gerald Bray. Contours of Christian Theology. Downers Grove: IVP, 1996.

Firth, David, and Paul D. Wegner, eds. *Presence, Power, and Promise: The Role of the Holy Spirit in the Old Testament.* Downers Grove, IL: IVP, 2011.

Gregory of Nazianzen, "Select Orations of Saint Gregory Nazianzen," in S. Cyril of Jerusalem, S. Gregory Nazianzen, ed. Philip Schaff and Henry Wace, trans. Charles Gordon Browne and James Edward Swallow, vol. 7 of *A Select Library of the Nicene and Post-Nicene Fathers of the Christian Church*, Second Series. New York: Christian Literature Company, 1894.

———. *Oration* 40, "On Holy Baptism," in Volume 41 of *A Select Library of the Nicene and Post-Nicene Fathers of the Christian Church.* Second Series. New York: Christian Literature Company, 1895.

Hamilton, James Jr. *God's Indwelling Presence: The Holy Spirit in the Old and New Testaments*. Nashville: B&H Academic, 2006.

Hamilton, Victor P. *Handbook on the Pentateuch*. 2nd ed. Grand Rapids: Baker Academic, 2005.

Holmes, Christopher R. J. *The Holy Spirit*. New Studies in Dogmatics. Edited by Michael Allen and Scott Swain. Grand Rapids: Zondervan, 2015.

Jones, Beth Felker. *God the Spirit: Introducing Pneumatology in Wesleyan and Ecumenical Perspective*. Edited by Randy Cooper et al. Volume 5 of *Wesleyan Doctrine Series*. Eugene, OR: Cascade Books, 2014.

Louth, Andrew. *Introducing Eastern Orthodox Theology*. London: SPCK, 2013.

Lyon, Robert W. "Baptism and Spirit-Baptism in the New Testament." Volume 14.1, Spring 1979 in *Wesleyan Theological Journal*, 14–26.

McCall, Thomas H. *Against God and Nature: The Doctrine of Sin*. Edited by John S. Feinberg, Foundations of Evangelical Theology. Wheaton, IL: Crossway, 2019.

———. "Chapter Three: Relational Trinity: Creedal Perspective," in *Two Views on the Doctrine of the Trinity*. Edited by Jason S. Sexton and Stanley N. Gundry. Zondervan Counterpoints Series Grand Rapids: Zondervan, 2014, 113–37.

Oden, Thomas C. *Life in the Spirit: Systematic Theology, Vol. III*. San Francisco: HarperSanFrancisco, 1992.

Olson, Roger E. *The Mosaic of Christian Belief: Twenty Centuries of Unity and Diversity*. 2nd ed. Downers Grove, IL: IVP Academic, 2016.

Olson, Roger E. and Christopher A. Hall. *The Trinity*. Guides to Theology. Grand Rapids: W. B. Eerdmans, 2002).

Otto, Rudolph. *The Idea of the Holy*. Oxford: Oxford University Press, 1958.

Peterson, Robert A. *Salvation Applied by the Spirit: Union with Christ*. Wheaton, IL: Crossway, 2015.

Schreiner, Thomas R. *Hebrews*. Edited by T. Desmond Alexander, Thomas R. Schreiner, and Andreas J. Köstenberger. Evangelical Biblical Theology. Bellingham, WA: Lexham Press, 2021.

Sexton, Jason S. and Stanley N. Gundry, eds. *Two Views on the Doctrine of the Trinity*. Zondervan Counterpoints Series. Grand Rapids: Zondervan, 2014.

Stott, John R. W. *Baptism and Fullness: The Work of the Holy Spirit Today*. 2nd ed. England: Inter-Varsity Press, 1975.

Tennent, Timothy C. *For the Body: Recovering a Theology of Gender, Sexuality, and the Human Body*. Grand Rapids: Zondervan, 2020.

Torrance, Thomas F. *The Christian Doctrine of God: One Being Three Persons*. New York: T&T Clark, 1996.

———. *The Trinitarian Faith: The Evangelical Theology of the Ancient Catholic Church*. 2nd ed. New York: T&T Clark, 1991.

Tozer, A. W. *The Pursuit of God*. Abbotsford, WI: Aneko Press, 2015.

Trites, Allison A. and William J. Larkin. *Cornerstone Biblical Commentary, Vol 12: The Gospel of Luke and Acts*. Carol Stream, IL: Tyndale House Publishers, 2006.

Turner, George Allen. "The Baptism of the Holy Spirit in the Wesleyan Tradition." Volume 14.1, Spring 1979 in *Wesleyan Theological Journal*, 60–76.

Vanhoozer, Kevin. *Biblical Authority after Babel: Retrieving the Solas in the Spirit of Mere Protestant Christianity*. Grand Rapids: Brazos Press, 2016.

Wesley, John. "Christian Perfection," in *The Sermons of John Wesley: A Collection for the Christian Journey*. Edited by Kenneth J. Collins and Jason E. Vickers. Nashville: Abingdon Press, 2013, 609–23.

———. "The Image of God," in *The Sermons of John Wesley: A Collection for the Christian Journey*. Edited by Kenneth J. Collins and Jason E. Vickers. Nashville: Abingdon Press, 2013, 1–9.

———. "Justification by Faith," in *The Sermons of John Wesley: A Collection for the Christian Journey*. Edited by Kenneth J. Collins and Jason E. Vickers. Nashville: Abingdon Press, 2013, 134–43.

———. "The Marks of the New Birth," in *The Sermons of John Wesley: A Collection for the Christian Journey*. Edited by Kenneth J. Collins and Jason E. Vickers. Nashville: Abingdon Press, 2013, 165–74.

———. "The Means of Grace." Sermon 12. https://www.umcdiscipleship.org/resources/john-wesley-on-the-means-of-grace.

———. "The New Birth," in *The Sermons of John Wesley: A Collection for the Christian Journey*. Edited by Kenneth J. Collins and Jason E. Vickers. Nashville: Abingdon Press, 2013, 155–64.

———. "On Working Out Our Own Salvation," in *The Sermons of John Wesley: A Collection for the Christian Journey*. Edited by Kenneth J. Collins and Jason E. Vickers. Nashville: Abingdon Press, 2013, 62–69.

———. "Original Sin," in *The Sermons of John Wesley: A Collection for the Christian Journey*. Edited by Kenneth J. Collins and Jason E. Vickers. Nashville: Abingdon Press, 2013, 10–19.

———. "The Scripture Way of Salvation," in *The Sermons of John Wesley: A Collection for the Christian Journey*. Edited by Kenneth J. Collins and Jason E. Vickers. Nashville: Abingdon Press, 2013, 581–90.

———. "The Witness of Our Own Spirit," in *The Sermons of John Wesley: A Collection for the Christian Journey*. Edited by Kenneth J. Collins and Jason E. Vickers. Nashville: Abingdon Press, 2013, 224–32.

———. "The Witness of the Spirit, I," in *The Sermons of John Wesley: A Collection for the Christian Journey*. Edited by Kenneth J. Collins and Jason E. Vickers. Nashville: Abingdon Press, 2013, 194–203.

Wright, N. T. "Romans" in *The New Interpreter's Bible: A Commentary in Twelve Volumes*. Volume 10. Nashville: Abingdon, 2015, 395–770.

Wynkoop, Mildred Bangs. "Theological Roots of the Wesleyan Understanding of the Holy Spirit." Volume 14.1, Spring 1979 in *Wesleyan Theological Journal*, 77–98.

Yadav, Sameer. "The Mystery of the Immanent Trinity and the Procession of the Spirit," in *The Third Person of the Trinity: Explorations in Constructive Dogmatics*. Edited by Oliver D. Crisp and Fred Sanders. Grand Rapids: Zondervan, 2020, 55–67.

Zizioulas, John. *Being as Communion: Studies in Personhood and the Church*. Crestwood, NY: St. Vladimir's Seminary Press 1985.

———. *Communion and Otherness: Further Studies in Personhood and the Church*. Edited by Paul McPartlan. New York: T&T Clark, 2006.

———. *Lectures in Church Dogmatics*. Edited by Douglas H. Knight. New York: T&T Clark, 2008.

SCRIPTURE INDEX

Acts
2	82, 98, 168, 169
2:1–4	82, 107
2:2–3	85
2:4	85
2:4, 8	170
2:33	85, 137
5:1–4	78
5:3	79
5:4	79
5:9	80
5:32	48
8:14–17	138
8:29	90
9	97
9:31	162, 165
10	194
11:18	116
13:2–3	90
15	40
15:28–29	88
17:28	70
21:8	170
21:11	90

Colossians
1:15–20	6
1:20	164
1:27	206

Daniel
7	52

Deuteronomy
4:2	36
5:7–8	49

Deuteronomy (continued)

6:4	31, 49
6:4–9	201
6:7	30
9:6	99
9:13	99
9:24	100
10:16	100
31:27	100
34:9	169

Ephesians

1:13	85, 189
1:14	85
2:4–5	128
2:15	164
4:5	159
4:11	170
4:17–24	107–8
4:18	108
4:30	87, 189
5:6	122

Exodus

2:2	169
3	1
3:5	1
3:14	2, 50, 69
19	82
20:8–11	36
31	168
32:9	99

Ezekiel

3:7	100
14:6	112
18:30	112
36:24–28	134
37	131
47:1–2	161

First Corinthians

1:7–8	175
1:30	142, 147
2:10	48, 89
2:10–11	72–73
2:13	22
3:16	80
6:11	80
6:17	153
6:19–20	80
10:13	208
12:3	104, 126, 158
12:4, 11	172
12:9	171
12:9, 28, 30	170
12:10	170, 171
12:13	153
12:28	171
13	171
13:1–3	171–72
13:8	173
13:8–13	175
14:1	170
15:23	191
15:51–57	153, 188

Scripture Index

First John
1:4–5	160
1:5–7	108–9
1:9	103, 123
2:2	117
3:9	129
3:10	167
3:15–16	160
3:20	26
4:2	170
4:4	74, 160, 207
4:6	80
4:7–21	11
4:10	114
4:13	153
5:1	130

First Kings
8:48	112
15:14	146

First Peter
1:2	141
1:11	80
1:21	90
4:10	170
5:8	32

First Samuel
1:3	73
2:2	2
4:3–5	203
16:13	169
25:37	135

First Thessalonians
4:16–17	188
5:16–18	145
5:23–24	146

First Timothy
2:13	103
3:16	53, 191
4:1	90

Galatians
2:16	124
4:6	149
6:8	161

Genesis
1:1	74, 130, 184
1:2	59, 80, 130
2:2	131
2:7	75
2:17	119
3	133
3:15	184
12:1–4	184
15	124
17:1	73
18:18	184
22:18	184

Hebrews
1:1–2	22
1:1–4	5
2:17	114

Hebrews (continued)

4:12	37
4:12–13	23–24
4:13	26
6:1	144
6:18	27
9:14	69
10:25	200
10:29	80, 88

Isaiah

1:5–6	121
1:27	113
6	119
11:2	80
11:2–3	169
40:13–17	73
40:17	72
40:28a	69
45:9–12	22–23
46:13	147
48:4	100
51:5	147
52:13–53:12	123
53:4–6	122
56:1	147
59:2	119
63:9	87
63:10	87

James

2:19	125
5:16	200

Jeremiah

23:23–24	70
31:31–33	134–35

Job

42:2	73

Joel

2:28–29	135–36

John

1:1	7, 69
1:4–5	75, 160
1:11–13	114
1:12–13	120, 130
1:14	8, 205
2	7, 150
2:21	7
3:1–8	139
3:5	75, 137
3:5–6	130
3:15–16	160
3:16	69, 116, 119
4:14	160
5:37–43	118
5:40	118
6:35	117
6:37	118
6:44	102, 115
6:63	75, 130
6:65	115
7:37b	118

7:37–38	160	**Leviticus**	
8:32	101	5:2–3	123
8:57–59	50		
8:58	69	**Luke**	
9:35–38	53	2:8–20	194
10:35	19	4:18	80
11:25	153	4:18–21	169
13:35	167	5:32	115
14:6	101	11:13	48, 199
14:9	6, 8, 48	11:38	151
14:10	58–59	12:7	71
14:15–17	136	13:3	113
14:16	48	15:7	115
14:17	80	20:34–40	153
14:17, 26	xii	22:19	200
14:20	59	24	47
14:25–27	162	24:27	19, 47
14:26	108, 162	24:46–47	117
15:18	165		
15:26	80	**Mark**	
16:7	91, 93	1:1–2	114
16:8	102, 104	1:7–8	152
16:13	80, 101	1:15	113
16:14	9, 48	2	7
16:22	136	2:5–7	51
17:1	48	2:15–17	195–96
17:5	69	9:43	119
20:1	197	13:11	90
20:22	48, 59, 75, 131	14:62–64	51–52
20:23	186		
21:15–19	98		

Matthew

1:18	75, 184
2:10–12	53
3:8	112
3:11	82, 136
3:16	80, 169
4:18–22	98
5:1–20	196
5:3	196
5:10	166
5:12	19
5:20	147
5:48	148, 207
6:5–15	200
6:16	200
6:24	113
10:30	26, 73
11:28	117
11:30	164
12:28–29	74
12:31–32	79, 103
14:33	53
15:17–20	135
16:13–20	98
16:17	158
16:18	158
16:22	136
16:25	116
18:20	200
21:42	19
22:29	19
22:43–44	22, 160
25:46	119
28:8–10	53
28:16–17	53
28:20	93

Micah

3:8	169

Nehemiah

9:30	22

Numbers

11:26	169
23:19	27

Philippians

1:6	145
2	116
2:1–11	167
2:2–4	181

Psalms

1	28, 200
1:2	201
1:3–4	201
7:12	113
19	5, 28, 200
19:7	30
22:3	200
33:6	59–60
43:10	69
51:10	130

51:10–11	134	1:20	73
51:11	81	2:5, 8	122
78:8	100	2:15	101
78:34	112	3:22	117
90	69	3:25	114
102:27	69	3:28	124
104:30	74	4:13	125
119	28, 200	5:1	164
121:4	69	5:5	189
133	167	5:9	123
139:7–8	81	5:12	119
139:7–12	71	5:19	185
147:4	26	6	189
147:5	26, 72	6:1–11	110, 129
		6:19	141
		6:22	142

Proverbs

3:19–20	72

Revelation

1:8	73
2:7	90
18–19	36
22:1–5	161
22:13	69
22:18–19	28–29

Romans

1:2	185, 191
1:1–4	52–53
1:4	75, 152
1:17	147
1:19	101

6:23	119, 164
7	188
7:5	109
7:9	109
7:25a	208
7–8	146
8	76
8:1	164
8:1–11	76–77
8:2	75, 76, 80, 164
8:6	76, 164
8:9	80, 189
8:10	76
8:11	76, 152–53
8:11, 16	xii
8:12–14	188

Romans (*continued*)
8:13	76
8:15–17	120
8:16	149
8:23	85
12:2	108
12:7	170, 171
12:8	170, 171
13:4–5	122
15:16	141

Second Corinthians
1:21–22	189
3:3	80
3:17	207
3:17–18	80
4:4	74, 101
5:1–9	153
5:17	128
5:21	147

Second Peter
1:20–21	22

Second Thessalonians
1:9	119
2:7	101
2:13	141
3:12	165

Second Timothy
2:25	116
3:16	37, 47
3:16–17	18, 21–22

Titus
1:2	26, 27
3:5	130

Printed by Libri Plureos GmbH in Hamburg, Germany